PACEMAKE

Practical
Mathematics
for Consumers

WORKBOOK

GLOBE FEARON

Pearson Learning Group

Pacemaker® Practical Mathematics for Consumers, Third Edition

We thank the following educators, who provided valuable comments and suggestions during the development of this book:

CONSULTANTS

Martha C. Beech, Center for Performance Technology, Florida State University, Tallahassee, Florida

Larry Timm, Special Education Teacher, Central Middle School, Midland, Michigan

REVIEWERS

Michael Brown, Department Chair, Mathematics, Hogan High School, Vallejo, California

Catherine Buckingham, Special Education Teacher, Friendly High School, Fort Washington, Maryland

PROJECT STAFF

Art and Design: Evelyn Bauer, Susan Brorein, Joan Jacobus, Jen Visco *Editorial:* Jane Books, Danielle Camaleri, Phyllis Dunsay, Elizabeth Fernald, Dena R. P. Kennedy *Manufacturing:* Mark Cirillo *Marketing:* Clare Harrison *Publishing Operations:* Travis Bailey, Debi Schlott

Copyright © 2004 by Pearson Education, Inc., publishing as Globe Fearon, Inc., an imprint of Pearson Learning Group, 299 Jefferson Road, Parsippany, New Jersey 07054. All rights reserved. No part of this book may be transmitted in any form or by any means, electronic or mechanical, including photocopying, recording, or by any information storage and retrieval system, without permission in writing from the publisher. For information regarding permission(s), write to Rights and Permissions Department.

ISBN: 0-13-024318-3

Printed in the United States of America

4 5 6 7 8 9 10   07 06 05

Globe Fearon
Pearson Learning Group

1-800-321-3106
www.pearsonlearning.com

Contents

A Note to Students   iv

Unit One
Chapter 1: Covering Your Expenses
Where Does Your Money Go?   Exercise 1
What Is an Expense Record?   Exercise 2
What Are Fixed and Variable
Expenses?   Exercise 3
What Is Income?   Exercise 4
How Do You Save for a Big
Expense?   Exercise 5

Chapter 2: Making and Changing Your Budget
What's in a Budget?   Exercise 6
Which Budget Items Can You
Change?   Exercise 7
How Do You Plan for Changes
in Your Budget?   Exercise 8
What Happens in Emergencies?   Exercise 9
How Do You Budget and Spend
Extra Money?   Exercise 10

Unit Two
Chapter 3: Your Salary
How Do You Calculate a Weekly,
Monthly, and Yearly Salary?   Exercise 11
How Do You Fill In a Time Card
and Calculate Overtime?   Exercise 12
How Do You Calculate Income
With Tips and Expenses
on the Job?   Exercise 13
How Do You Calculate a Salary
With Commission?   Exercise 14

Chapter 4: Your Take-home Pay
How Do You Find Net Pay?   Exercise 15
How Do You Find a Percent of
Gross Pay?   Exercise 16
What Percent of Gross Pay Is
Each Deduction?   Exercise 17
How Do You Read a Tax Table?   Exercise 18
What Is Health Insurance?   Exercise 19
How Can You Save Money and
Plan for Retirement?   Exercise 20

Unit Three
Chapter 5: Choosing a Bank
How Do You Choose a Bank
That Is Best for You?   Exercise 21
How Do You Calculate Bank Fees?   Exercise 22
How Much Interest Do You Earn?   Exercise 23

Chapter 6: Using a Checking Account
How Do You Deposit Money?   Exercise 24
How Do You Fill Out a
WithdrawalSlip?   Exercise 25
Hoe Do You Write a Check?   Exercise 26
How Do You Keep Track of
Your Account Balance?   Exercise 27
What Is a Bank Statement?   Exercise 28
Do You Reconcile Your Account
Correctly?   Exercise 29

Unit Four
Chapter 7: Credit Card Math
Do You Want a Credit Card?   Exercise 30
How Do You Open a Credit
Card Account?   Exercise 31
How Do You Protect Your
Credit Card?   Exercise 32
What About Buying on Credit?   Exercise 33
How Do You Read a Monthly
Statement?   Exercise 34
What Happens When You Return
an Item?   Exercise 35
Should You Continue to Buy
on Credit?   Exercise 36
What Is a Cash Advance?   Exercise 37

Chapter 8: Loans and Interest
Where Can You Get a Loan?   Exercise 38
What Will the Loan Cost?   Exercise 39
What Is on a Loan Application?   Exercise 40
What Is the Fee on a Loan?   Exercise 41

Unit Five
Chapter 9: FInding a Place to Live
How Much Can You Afford for
Rent?   Exercise 42
How Do You FInd the Place
You Need?   Exercise 43
What Is in a Lease?   Exercise 44
What Is a Security Deposit?   Exercise 45
Can You Afford to Buy a House?   Exercise 46
How Much Is the Down
Payment?   Exercise 47
How Much Is the Monthly
Mortgage Payment?   Exercise 48
What About Closing Costs?   Exercise 49
What Is Real Estate Tax?   Exercise 50
What About Homeowner's
Insurance?   Exercise 51

Chapter 10: Decorating Your Home

How Can You Furnish Your Home on a Limited Budget?   Exercise 52

Should You Buy on Sale?   Exercise 53

What Appliances Should You Buy? Exercise 54

Which Plan Is Best for You?   Exercise 55

How Much Paint Will You Need?   Exercise 56

How Many Tiles Do You Need to Cover the Floor?   Exercise 57

Unit Six

Chapter 11: Eating for Good Health

What Is a Balanced Diet?   Exercise 58

What Can I Do If I Do Not Eat Some Foods?   Exercise 59

What Are Calories?   Exercise 60

How Do You Burn Calories? and What's Wrong With Fat, Salt, and Sugar?   Exercise 61

Chapter 12: Choosing and Buying Groceries

What Do Labels Tell You?   Exercise 62

How Can You Save Money By Comparing Prices?   Exercise 63

How Can Coupons Save You Money?   Exercise 64

Are You a Wise Shopper?   Exercise 65

Unit Seven

Chapter 13: Deciding What You Need

How Do You Calculate Sales Tax on Items You Really Need?   Exercise 66

Which Clothes Do You Need?   Exercise 67

What About Personal Care?   Exercise 68

Is a Sales Item Always a Better Buy?   Exercise 69

Is This Advertisement Misleading? Exercise 70

Can You Believe What You Read?   Exercise 71

Chapter 14: Getting the Best Buy

When Are Items On Sale?   Exercise 72

How Do You Find the Sales Price? Exercise 73

How Do You Place a Catalog Order?   Exercise 74

How Do You Find the Total Cost of Your Order?   Exercise 75

Unit Eight

Chapter 15: Buying and Leasing a Vehicle

What Kind of Transportation Will Save You Money?   Exercise 76

What About Shopping for a Reliable Car?   Exercise 77

How Do You Pay for a Car?   Exercise 78

How Do You Check the Contract? Exercise 79

What About Making Car Loan Payments?   Exercise 80

What About Leasing a Vehicle?   Exercise 81

Chapter 16: Maintaining a Vehicle

What About Car Insurance?   Exercise 82

How Does a Deductible Work?   Exercise 83

How Do You Keep Your Vehicle Running?   Exercise 84

What About Car Repairs?   Exercise 85

Unit Nine

Chapter 17: Budgeting for Recreation

How Much Does Recreation Cost? Exercise 86

How Can Bargains Save You Money?   Exercise 87

How Can Comparing Prices Save You Money?   Exercise 88

How Can You Budget for Recreation Costs?   Exercise 89

Chapter 18: Planning a Trip

How Long Will the Trip Take?   Exercise 90

How Much Will Gasoline Cost?   Exercise 91

How Much Will Food and Lodging Cost?   Exercise 92

A Note to the Student

The exercises in this workbook go along with your *Pacemaker® Practical Mathematics for Consumers* textbook. This workbook will give you a chance to review concepts you learned in your textbook, to practice skills, and to think critically.

Set goals for yourself and try to meet them as you complete each activity. The more you practice, the more you will remember. Being able to remember and apply information is a skill that will help you succeed in school, at work, and in life.

By completing the activities in this workbook, you will learn a lot about mathematics skills you can use everyday.

Name _____ Date _____

 1 ▶ **Where Does Your Money Go?**   **Exercise 1**

Lesson 1.1

Eli made a list to show how he spent his money one week.
Use Eli's list to solve each problem.

SPENT DURING WEEK OF JANUARY 19ᵀᴴ

Car payment *$159.99*   Magazine subscription *$15.36*
Gasoline *$18.50*   Video game *$25.79*
Monthly parking pass *$45.00*   Groceries *$75.44*
New school books *$148.06*   Shirt *$20.50*

---

1. Fill in the needs and wants chart using the items from Eli's list.

Need	Cost

Want	Cost

2. Which item that Eli needed cost the least?

3. Which item that Eli wanted cost the most?

4. In which chart did you place the shirt, the needs chart or the wants chart? Explain your thinking.

5. In which chart did you place the new school books, the needs chart or the wants chart? Explain your thinking.

MAINTAINING SKILLS

Circle the greater amount in each pair.

   1. $67 $65   **2.** $58.07 $60.45   **3.** $101.90 $99.16

   4. $99.80 $99.85   **5.** $44.37 $44.22   **6.** $30 $29.99

Pacemaker ® Practical Mathematics for Consumers© Pearson Education, Inc. / Globe Fearon / Pearson Learning Group. All rights reserved.

Name _____   Date _____

 1 ▷ What Is an Expense Record?   **Exercise 2**

Lesson 1.3

Zack made one expense record to show how he spent his money during the
past four weeks. Use Zack's expense record to solve each problem.

Zack's Expense Record				
Category	Week 1	Week 2	Week 3	Week 4
Food	$50.00	$43.00	$29.00	$48.00
Clothing	$74.50	$29.25		
Transportation	$18.00	$15.00	$9.00	$25.00
Personal care	$15.00	$30.00	$25.00	$10.00
Recreation	$10.00	$9.00	$20.00	$20.00
Utilities		$37.55	$42.75	
Health insurance				$78.00
Rent				$400.00
Savings	$25.00	$75.00	$100.00	$100.00
Other	$62.50	$48.95	$38.43	$26.25

1. How much money did Zack put into savings this month?

2. For which category did Zack spend the least amount of money?

3. Did Zack spend more on food or on clothing for the month? How
much more?

4. Did Zack spend more money in week 1 or in week 4? How much more?

MAINTAINING SKILLS

Add.

1. $191.23
       + 25.58

2. $264.78
       + 95.25

3. $760.06
       + 848.95

4. $1,943.90
       + 79.97

5. $893.85 + $50.69 = _____

6. $1,913.74 + $98.87 = _____

Pacemaker ® Practical Mathematics for Consumers© Pearson Education, Inc. / Globe Fearon / Pearson Learning Group. All rights reserved.

Name _____ Date _____

 1 ▶ **What Are Fixed and Variable Expenses?**　　Exercise 3

Lesson 1.4

The list below shows Linda's expenses for one month. Use Linda's list to solve each problem.

MONEY SPENT IN JUNE

Rent $350.00　　　　　　Gasoline $48.90

Car payment $144.00　　Clothing $110.00

Car insurance $81.00　　Recreation $65.00

Utilities $52.25　　　　　Telephone $54.18

Groceries $160.00　　　Personal care $22.48

---

1. Fill in the fixed expense and the variable expense charts. The first one is done for you.

Fixed Expense	Cost	
Rent		$350.00

Variable Expense	Cost

2. Did Linda spend more of her income on fixed expenses or variable expenses in June? How much more?

3. Linda has $1,600 to spend for the month. Add all her expenses. Will she have any money left over? How much?

MAINTAINING SKILLS

Subtract.

1.	$38.03	2.	$43.90	3.	$848.95	4.	$1,312.45
	− 29.25		− 9.97		− 96.97		− 423.37

Pacemaker ® Practical Mathematics for Consumers© Pearson Education, Inc. / Globe Fearon / Pearson Learning Group. All rights reserved.

Name _____   Date _____

1 ▶ What Is Income?   Exercise 4

Lesson 1.5

Solve each problem. Show your work.

1. Sharon earns $2,109 per month. Her fixed expenses for the month are $1,590. How much money does Sharon have left for variable expenses each month?

2. Tom's income is $1,980.72 per month. His fixed expenses for the month are $1,518.44. How much money does Tom have left for variable expenses each month?

3. Tawanda earns $954 per week. Her fixed expenses for the week are $590. How much money does Tawanda have left for variable expenses each week?

4. Jacob's income is $980.72 per week. His fixed expenses for the week are $542.67. How much money does Jacob have left for variable expenses each week?

5. Tyrone's income is $985.86 per week. His fixed expenses for the week are $529.52. His variable expenses are $336.04. How much money does Tyrone have left for savings each week?

MAINTAINING SKILLS

Add or subtract.

1. $96.47
  − 7.29
	2. $23.54
	  + 3.65
		3. $40.67
		  − 9.42
			4. $72.56
			  + 29.37

5. $263.79 − $63.89 = _____   6. $174.36 + $25.67 = _____

Pacemaker ® Practical Mathematics for Consumers© Pearson Education, Inc. / Globe Fearon / Pearson Learning Group. All rights reserved.

Name _____ Date _____

 How Do You Save for a Big Expense?   **Exercise 5**

Lesson 1.7

Solve each problem. Show your work.

1. Natalie saves $35 each month to buy a DVD player. The DVD player costs $197.99. Will Natalie be able to buy the DVD player in 5 months? If not, how much more money does she need?

2. Lisa has $375 in savings for an exercise machine. The exercise machine costs $660. She wants to buy the exercise machine in four months. She wants to save the same amount every month. How much would she have to save every month?

3. You want to buy a computer. The computer costs $1,200. How much would you have to save every month for 6 months to be able to buy the computer? For 8 months?

4. Ken has $340 in his savings account. He wants to buy a new stereo for $800. If he saves $125 a month for the next five months, will he have enough to buy this stereo? If yes, how much savings will he have left after the purchase?

MAINTAINING SKILLS

Multiply or divide.

1. $4)\overline{\$65.00}$

2. $5)\overline{\$110.40}$

3. $\begin{array}{r} \$760.00 \\ \times\ \ 79.97 \\ \hline \end{array}$

4. $\$48.21 \times 3 =$ _____

5. $\$78.04 \times 3 =$ _____

Pacemaker ® Practical Mathematics for Consumers© Pearson Education, Inc. / Globe Fearon / Pearson Learning Group. All rights reserved.

2 ▶ What's In a Budget?

Lesson 2.1

Eva shares an apartment with one roommate. She earns a monthly income of $1,000. Eva and her roommate share all expenses equally.

Eva's Shared Expenses			
Fixed Expense	**Cost**	**Variable Expense**	**Cost**
Rent	$500.00	Utilities	$75.00
Cable TV	$25.00	Phone	$43.00

Use the information above and the chart to complete Exercises 1–4. Show your work.

1. Eva's share of the rent is $500 a month. She pays the same amount as her roommate. How much is the total cost of rent each month?

2. What is the total of Eva's monthly fixed expenses for the apartment?

3. After Eva pays her shared expenses, how much money does she have left for savings and other expenses?

4. Suppose the cable TV bill increases by $5.60 a month. How much would Eva's share be then?

MAINTAINING SKILLS

Add or subtract.

1. $32.87
   + 10.32

2. $16.00
   + 7.21

3. $91.45
   − 19.31

4. $55.55
   − 33.33

5. $68.05 + $40.25 = _____

6. $25.00 − $16.50 = _____

Pacemaker ® Practical Mathematics for Consumers© Pearson Education, Inc. / Globe Fearon / Pearson Learning Group. All rights reserved.

Name _____ Date _____

2 ▸ Which Budget Items Can You Change? — Exercise 7

Lesson 2.2

Use José's monthly budget to solve each problem.

José's Monthly Budget			
Monthly Income			$1,250
Expenses			
Rent	$540	Gas	$80
Utilities	$95	Tolls	$60
Recreation	$150	Car Insurance	$105
Savings			$220

1. José must add $15 to gas, $10 to tolls, and $55 to car insurance. Is there enough money in recreation to transfer for these expenses? If yes, how much will be left?

2. Make the transfers suggested in Problem 1. Show what José's new budget will look like.

3. Suppose José buys a computer. He will pay $125 a month for one year. He decides to subtract the expense from his savings. Now what will be the amount of his savings each month?

MAINTAINING SKILLS

Add or subtract.

1. $106.10
    −   56.05

2. $25.75
    − 13.37

3. $48.26
    + 27.12

4. $87.65
    + 81.75

5. 99 + 12 + 15 = _____

6. 200 − 95 = _____

Pacemaker ® Practical Mathematics for Consumers© Pearson Education, Inc. / Globe Fearon / Pearson Learning Group. All rights reserved.

Name _____ Date _____

2 ▷ How Do You Plan for Changes in Your Budget?

Lessons 2.4 and 2.5

You are planning to go to a wedding next year. You will need to save $100 a month to have enough money for travel and a gift. Your rent is increasing by $50 a month. However, you made your last car payment of $209 this month.

Budget Changes	
Expenses Added to Budget	**Expenses Subtracted from Budget**
• $100 a month for wedding travel and gift • $50 a month rent increase	• $209 a month for car payment

Use the information and the budget above to complete Exercises 1–4.

1. What is the total of the expenses you will add to your monthly budget?

2. What is the total of the expenses you will subtract from your budget?

3. Which is greater, the expenses you will add or the expenses you will subtract? How much greater?

4. Now can you afford not to save $65 a month for tennis lessons? Explain.

_____

_____

MAINTAINING SKILLS

Estimate each sum or difference. Round to the nearest dollar. Then add or subtract.

1.	$27.51 − 13.41	2.	$43.78 + 9.50	3.	$73.12 + 26.99	4.	$65.65 − 43.81

Pacemaker ® Practical Mathematics for Consumers© Pearson Education, Inc. / Globe Fearon / Pearson Learning Group. All rights reserved.

Name _____ Date _____

Lesson 2.6

Your car will not start. The repair shop charges you $95 to tow the car. To repair the car will cost $430. The car won't be ready for one week.

Lucky for you, your roommate lends you a bicycle. You ride the bicycle to work, but it is stolen. Now you owe your roommate $150 to replace the bicycle.

Use the information above to answer each question.
Show your work.

1. How much extra money do you need this month to cover these emergencies?

2. You have only $150 in savings. So you decide to pay your roommate for the bicycle. What is your total debt now?

3. The repair shop agreed to let you pay off your debt monthly. How long will it take to pay off your debt if you pay $60 a month?

MAINTAINING SKILLS

Compute.

1. $52.16
   $\times$ 21

2. $89.20
   $\times$ 7

3. 7)$142.45

4. $45
      16
   +   9

5. $10.45 ÷ 5 = _____

6. $496.25 − $86.00 = _____

Pacemaker ® Practical Mathematics for Consumers© Pearson Education, Inc. / Globe Fearon / Pearson Learning Group. All rights reserved.

Name _____ Date _____

Lessons 2.8 and 2.9

Ella's monthly income is $1,575. She likes to swim and decides to join RCS Pool Club. Club dues are $600 a year.

Ella's New Monthly Budget

Monthly Income	$1,575
Fixed Expenses	
Rent	$425
Cable TV	$30
Car insurance	$120
RCS Pool Club ① [ ]	
Variable Expenses	
Groceries	$150
Utilities	$90
Clothing	$100
Recreation	$200
Savings	
Savings for gifts and emergencies ② [ ]	
Total	$1,575

Use the information and the budget above to answer each question. Show your work.

1. Ella decides to pay for her pool club membership monthly. How much will she pay each month? Write this amount in Ella's budget above.

2. What is the total amount of money Ella has for savings each month? Write this amount in Ella's budget above.

3. Ella gets a job at the pool club. She is paid $10 an hour and works 4 hours a week. By how much will Ella's monthly income increase?

MAINTAINING SKILLS

Multiply or divide.

1. $75
   $\times\ 5$

2. $8)\overline{\$5,632}$

3. 640
   $\times\ 4$

4. $10)\overline{750}$

Pacemaker ® Practical Mathematics for Consumers© Pearson Education, Inc. / Globe Fearon / Pearson Learning Group. All rights reserved.

Name _____ Date _____

Lessons 3.1 and 3.2

Use the employment ads below to solve each problem. Show your work. Round to the nearest cent if necessary.

> **Receptionist** for a busy law firm. Salary $26,000/year. Must have good phone skills and organizational skills. Overtime available. 40 hrs/wk.

> **Daycare Worker**–no experience necessary. 40 hr/wk, $10/hr. Good people skills necessary. Must be available 5 days/wk, 8 hr/day.

1. How much is the daycare worker paid for a 40-hour work week?

2. How much is the receptionist paid for a 40-hour work week?

3. How much more is the receptionist paid for a 40-hour work week than the daycare worker?

4. You took the job as the daycare worker. After the first year, you got a $2 per hour raise. What is your new hourly wage? Weekly salary? Yearly salary?

MAINTAINING SKILLS

Compute.

1. $42.51
   + 19.25

2. $25.91
   − 8.72

3. $27.31
   + 19.31

4. $11.35
   × 4

5. 5)16.50

6. $54.69
   − 33.21

7. $68.90
   × 7

8. 8)32.48

Pacemaker ® Practical Mathematics for Consumers© Pearson Education, Inc. / Globe Fearon / Pearson Learning Group. All rights reserved.

Name _____ Date _____

 3 ▶ How Do You Fill In a Time Card and Calculate Overtime?   **Exercise 12**

Lessons 3.3 and 3.4

Joe works at C & J Auto Repair. Joe gets paid overtime for any hours over 40 hours per week. Overtime is paid as time and a half.

Use the information above and Joe's time card to find the total hours Joe worked each day. Write your answers in the chart.

	Name: Joe Temming **Hourly Rate:** $10			**Job Title:** Mechanic **Week Ending:** 1/11		
	Day	**Date**	**Time In**	**Time Out**	**Break**	**Total**
1.	Monday	1/6	7 A.M.	6 P.M.	$\frac{1}{2}$ hour	
2.	Tuesday	1/7	7 A.M.	7 P.M.	1 hour	
3.	Wednesday	1/8	9 A.M.	4 P.M.	0	
4.	Thursday	1/9	8 A.M.	5 P.M.	$\frac{1}{2}$ hour	
5.	Friday	1/10	7 A.M.	4 P.M.	1 hour	

Use the information in Joe's time card to solve each problem.

6. How many hours did Joe work this week? _____

7. On average, how long did Joe work each day? _____

8. How much was Joe paid for total overtime this week? _____

9. How much did Joe earn this week? _____

MAINTAINING SKILLS

Find the average.

1. $30, $45, $15 _____

2. $18, $93, $34, $45 _____

3. $9, $4, $5, $8, $10 _____

Pacemaker ® Practical Mathematics for Consumers© Pearson Education, Inc. / Globe Fearon / Pearson Learning Group. All rights reserved.

Name _____ Date _____

 How Do You Calculate Income With Tips and Expenses On the Job? **Exercise 13**

Lessons 3.5 and 3.6

Find the weekly income for each employee. Write each answer in the chart.

	Employee	Hourly Wage	Hours Worked	Weekly Tips	Weekly Income
1.	Jack	$7.61	25	$380	
2.	Melinda	$8.25	36	$100	
3.	Sinu	$6.45	20	$125	
4.	Aaron	$9.00	38	$250	

Use the information in the chart above to solve each problem.

5. As a valet, Jack must wear a uniform. He spends $6 a week to have his uniform cleaned. He also drives to work and spends about $25 a week in gas and tolls. What is his weekly income after paying these expenses?

6. Sinu must wear a uniform shirt to work each day. She spends $10 a week to have the shirts cleaned. What is her monthly income after paying these expenses?

MAINTAINING SKILLS

Compute.

1. $15.32
      ×   10

2. $25.98
      + 77.23

3. $123.75
      − 87.25

4. 6)$99.36

Pacemaker ® Practical Mathematics for Consumers© Pearson Education, Inc. / Globe Fearon / Pearson Learning Group. All rights reserved.

Name _____ Date _____

3 ► How Do You Calculate a Salary With Commission?

Exercise 14

Lessons 3.8 and 3.9

 Find each commission. Then find each total income. Write each answer in the chart.

	Salesperson	Amount of Sales	Rate of Commission	Commission	Weekly Salary	Total Income
1.	Kathy	$5,280	1.5%		$530	
2.	Melissa	$4,361	3%		$379	
3.	David	$8,411	5%		$716	
4.	Jennifer	$10,620	3.5%		$291	
5.	Peter	$5,000	2.5%		$605	

Use the information in the chart above to solve each problem.

6. If Peter's weekly sales tripled, what would be his commission?

7. Suppose Jennifer's rate of commission increased to 4%. How much more money would she make in commission each week?

MAINTAINING SKILLS

Write each percent as a decimal.

1. 30% _____

2. 27% _____

3. 6% _____

Find the percent of each number.

4. 3% of $1,231 _____

5. 45% of $631 _____

6. 10% of $100 _____

7. 25% of $250 _____

Pacemaker ® Practical Mathematics for Consumers© Pearson Education, Inc. / Globe Fearon / Pearson Learning Group. All rights reserved.

Name _____ Date _____

 4 ▶ **How Do You Find Net Pay?** **Exercise 15**

Lessons 4.1 and 4.2

Sue is an office assistant. This is her biweekly earnings statement.

Name: Sue Brown **Social Security Number:** 000-99-0009

Gross Pay	Federal Tax	State Tax	FICA	Medicare	Health Insurance	Union Dues	Net Pay
$700.00	$102.00	$21.60	$37.68	$10.50	$31.75	$8.20	

 Use the earnings statement above to solve each problem. Show your work.

1. What is the total amount of deductions taken from Sue's gross pay?

2. What is Sue's net pay?

3. How much does Sue pay in union dues each year?

4. New Hampshire has no state income tax. If Sue lived in New Hampshire, what would her yearly net pay be?

MAINTAINING SKILLS

Multiply.

1. $48
× 20

2. $3.60
× 12

3. $432
× 52

4. $512
× 10

5. $56.12 × 10 = _____

6. $294 × 26 = _____

Pacemaker ® Practical Mathematics for Consumers© Pearson Education, Inc. / Globe Fearon / Pearson Learning Group. All rights reserved.

Name _____   Date _____

Lesson 4.3

Use the circle graph to solve each problem. Show your work.

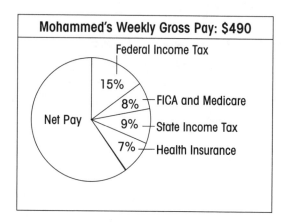

1. What is Mohammed's net pay each week?

2. What percent of Mohammed's gross pay is his net pay?

3. How much does Mohammed pay for health insurance each week?

4. How much does Mohammed pay each week for state income tax and federal income tax altogether?

MAINTAINING SKILLS

Divide to find the percent.

1. $\frac{1}{100}$ _____   2. $\frac{6}{10}$ _____   3. $\frac{50}{80}$ _____   4. $\frac{6}{200}$ _____

Write each as a percent.

5. $42 out of $100 _____   6. $18 out of $300 _____

Pacemaker ® Practical Mathematics for Consumers© Pearson Education, Inc. / Globe Fearon / Pearson Learning Group. All rights reserved.

Name _____   Date _____

Lesson 4.5

The circle graph shows Carrie's weekly gross pay,
her deductions, and her net pay.

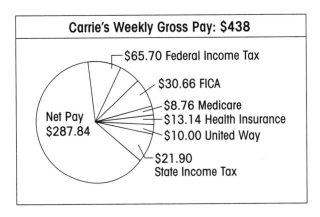

Carrie's Weekly Gross Pay: $438

$65.70 Federal Income Tax
$30.66 FICA
$8.76 Medicare
$13.14 Health Insurance
$10.00 United Way
$21.90 State Income Tax
Net Pay $287.84

Use the circle graph to solve each problem. Show your work.

1. Which deduction takes the greatest percent of Carrie's gross
   pay? The least?

2. What percent of Carrie's gross pay is taken for Social Security?
   (Hint: FICA is Social Security)

3. What percent of Carrie's gross pay is taken for income tax?
   (Hint: Find the percent of state income tax and the percent of
   federal income tax. Then add.)

4. What percent of Carrie's gross pay is her net pay?
   Round to the nearest whole percent.

MAINTAINING SKILLS

Write each as a percent.

1. $60 out of $300 _____   2. $120 out of $625 _____

3. $6 out of $15 _____   4. $7 out of $28 _____

Pacemaker ® Practical Mathematics for Consumers© Pearson Education, Inc. / Globe Fearon / Pearson Learning Group. All rights reserved.

Name _____ Date _____

 4 ▶ **How Do You Read a Tax Table?** **Exercise 18**

Lessons 4.6, 4.7, and 4.8

Solve each problem. Show your work.

1. Lamont makes $28,300 a year. This year, he earned $100 in interest from his savings account. He has $6,800 in exemptions for his dependents. He also has $5,000 in deductions. What is his taxable income?

2. Celeste makes $26,500 a year. Her exemptions total $1,400. She can deduct $3,800 for business expenses. What is her taxable income?

If your taxable income is —		And you are —			
At least	But less than	Single	Married filing jointly	Married filing separately	Head of a household
		Your tax is —			
$23,000	$23,050	3,154	2,854	3,154	2,954
$23,050	$23,100	3,161	2,861	3,161	2,961

Find the refund or balance due for each person in the chart below. Use the information in the tax table above for Problems 3–5.

	Name	Status	Taxable Income	Total Federal Tax Withheld	Refund	Balance Due
3.	Martin	Head of household	$23,030	$3,210		
4.	Pang	Single	$23,075	$3,000		
5.	Ruby	Married filing separately	$23,092	$3,010		

MAINTAINING SKILLS

Write each decimal as a percent.

1. 0.27 _____   2. 0.025 _____   3. 1.25 _____   4. 0.63 _____

Pacemaker ® Practical Mathematics for Consumers© Pearson Education, Inc. / Globe Fearon / Pearson Learning Group. All rights reserved.

Name _____ Date _____

 4 ▷ **What Is Health Insurance?**   **Exercise 19**

Lesson 4.9

Use the chart below to solve each problem. Show your work.

Coverage Choices for Health Insurance	
People Covered	**Cost Per Month**
Employee	$20.95
Employee and spouse	$25.50
Employee and family	$43.20

1. Jane is starting a new job and choosing a health plan. What will the health insurance cost Jane each year if she is single?

2. Victor recently got married and wants to include his wife on his health insurance. If he chooses the employee and spouse plan, how much will he spend each year on health benefits?

3. Emily is choosing a health plan. She has three children. What is the best plan for Emily? How much will she pay each month?

4. Toby is married with two children. He pays $518.40 a year for health insurance. Which plan does Toby have? How much does this plan cost per month?

MAINTAINING SKILLS

Multiply.

1. $162.15
   $\times$ 12

2. $54.21
   $\times$ 7

3. $49.49
   $\times$ 6

4. $16.15 $\times$ 9 = _____

Pacemaker ® Practical Mathematics for Consumers© Pearson Education, Inc. / Globe Fearon / Pearson Learning Group. All rights reserved.

Name _____ Date _____

4 ▶ How Can You Save Money and Plan for Retirement?

Exercise 20

Lessons 4.10 and 4.11

Solve each problem. Show your work.

1. Alfonso wants to buy a $500 Series EE savings bond. How much will he pay for the bond?

2. Alfonso bought one $50 Series EE bond every month for one year. How much did Alfonso pay for all his bonds? What is the total amount the bonds will be worth when they mature?

Use the information in the monthly earnings statement to solve Problems 3–5. Show your work. Round to the nearest cent.

Name: Alfonso Ruiz   **Social Security Number:** 000-99-0099

Gross Pay	Federal Tax	State Tax	FICA	Medicare	401(k)	Net Pay
$2,324.58	$348.69	$92.98	$139.47	$46.49	$116.23	$1,580.72

3. Alfonso uses a payroll deduction to deposit $120 into his savings account each month. How much will he save in a year?

4. If Alfonso increased his 401(k) plan contribution to 7%, how much would be deducted each month for retirement?

5. Alfonso's employer pays $0.50 for every $1.00 of Alfonso's contribution to his 401(k) plan. How much is the employer's contribution to Alfonso's retirement fund each month?

MAINTAINING SKILLS

Write each percent as a decimal.

1. 1% _____   2. 50% _____   3. 16% _____

4. 4.25% _____   5. 6.3% _____   6. 175% _____

Pacemaker ® Practical Mathematics for Consumers® Pearson Education, Inc. / Globe Fearon / Pearson Learning Group. All rights reserved.

Name _____ Date _____

Lessons 5.1 and 5.2

Solve each problem. Show your work.

1. Wilmer cashed his paycheck at Check Express. The fee at Check Express is 9% of the amount of the check. His paycheck was $291. How much was the fee for Wilmer to cash his paycheck?

2. Ashanti cashed her paycheck at Cash-n-Go. The fee at Cash-n-Go is 7.5% of the amount of the check. Her paycheck was $670. How much was the fee for Ashanti to cash her paycheck?

Use the information in the chart below to solve Problems 3 and 4.

Bank Services		
Services	Appleseed Bank	American Bank
Monthly service charge for checking accounts	$3	Free
Monthly service charge for savings accounts	$5	Free
Direct deposit	Yes	No
Open late one night and Saturdays	Yes	No

3. If Alex chooses Appleseed Bank, how much will he pay a year for a checking account? A savings account?

4. Which bank would be best for Alex if he can only go to the bank in the evening, and if he wants direct deposit?

MAINTAINING SKILLS

Write each percent as a decimal.

1. 5% _____   2. 62% _____   3. 0.07% _____

4. 11.3% _____   5. 7.25% _____   6. 126% _____

Pacemaker ® Practical Mathematics for Consumers© Pearson Education, Inc. / Globe Fearon / Pearson Learning Group. All rights reserved.

Name _____ Date _____

Lessons 5.3 and 5.4

Use the chart below to solve Problems 1 and 2. Show your work.

Checking Accounts at Appleseed Bank			
	Checking Account A	**Checking Account B**	**Checking Account C**
Check fee	$0.50 on each check	First 6 checks a month are free, then $0.60 a check	Free
Debit card fee	Free at branch; $1.50 at any other bank	Free at branch; $1.00 at any other bank	First 5 times a month free at any bank; $0.75 for each additional use
Monthly service charge	$4.00	Free	$6.00

1. Anna expects to write 9 checks a month. Which checking account is best for Anna?

2. Joel expects to write 15 checks a month. He has Checking Account A. How much will Joel pay for his checking account each month?

Solve. Show your work.

3. Caitlin used the ATM at her bank to withdraw $220. Before she used the ATM, her balance was $437.60. Caitlin's bank does not charge account holders an ATM fee. What is her new balance?

MAINTAINING SKILLS

Add or subtract.

1. $345
    + 26

2. $567.82
    − 28.98

3. $1,200.67
    − 349.98

4. $82 + $26 + $29 = _____

Pacemaker ® Practical Mathematics for Consumers© Pearson Education, Inc. / Globe Fearon / Pearson Learning Group. All rights reserved.

Name _____ Date _____

Lessons 5.5 and 5.6

Find the simple interest earned.

	Principal	Interest Rate	Period of Time	Simple Interest
1.	$5,625	2.6%	2 years	
2.	$4,100	1.25%	3 years	
3.	$2,360	4.5%	5 years	
4.	$1,500	3%	7 years	

 Find the total value of the CD when it matures. Round to the nearest cent.

	Principal	Period of Time	Interest Rate	When Compounded	Value at Maturity
5.	$3,200	3 months	3.75%	quarterly	
6.	$2,700	6 months	2.5%	semiannually	
7.	$4,150	9 months	4%	quarterly	
8.	$1,000	6 months	3%	quarterly	

MAINTAINING SKILLS

Write each percent as a decimal.

1. 3.5% _____   **2.** 1.25% _____   **3.** 2.5% _____

4. 9% _____   **5.** 7.8% _____   **6.** 0.2% _____

7. 3.6% _____   **8.** 0.65% _____   **9.** 107% _____

Pacemaker ® Practical Mathematics for Consumers© Pearson Education, Inc. / Globe Fearon / Pearson Learning Group. All rights reserved.

Name _____ Date _____

Lessons 6.1 and 6.2

Mark deposits an $80.00 check, a $52.00 check, and $8.25 in coins into his checking account. He takes $25.00 in cash back.

<table>
<tr><td rowspan="11" style="writing-mode:vertical-rl">DEPOSIT TICKET
PLEASE PRESS FIRMLY</td></tr>
</table>

Mark Gray 172 32nd Street Omaha, NE 68005	① CASH	CURRENCY		
		COIN		
DATE *November 11, 2003* DEPOSITS MAY NOT BE AVAILABLE FOR IMMEDIATE WITHDRAWAL	LIST CHECKS SINGLY			55-555/1234 7654321
_____ SIGN HERE FOR CASH RECEIVED (IF REQUIRED)	② TOTAL			
Lion Bank 95 Main Street Omaha, Nebraska 68005	LESS CASH RECEIVED ③ NET DEPOSIT			BE SURE EACH ITEM IS PROPERLY ENDORSED

⑈087123528⑈ 865296124

Use the information above to complete Exercises 1–3.

1. On the deposit slip, list Mark's deposits.

2. What is Mark's total deposit? Write this amount on the deposit slip.

3. What is Mark's net deposit? Write this amount on the deposit slip.

Answer the question.

4. How does the bank know if Mark is actually the account holder? Explain.

_____

_____

_____

MAINTAINING SKILLS

Write each percent as a fraction in simplest form.

1. 40% _____   2. 20% _____   3. 38% _____   4. 5% _____

Pacemaker ® Practical Mathematics for Consumers© Pearson Education, Inc. / Globe Fearon / Pearson Learning Group. All rights reserved.

Name _____ Date _____

Lesson 6.3

Answer each question.

1. Suppose you need to withdraw $115 in cash from your account today to buy school clothes. Fill out the withdrawal slip below.

WITHDRAWAL   Date _____

    Pay to the Order Of _____ By ☐ Cash
                                         ☐ Check

    For _____ Dollars ($ _____)

    TO BE CHARGED TO MY ACCOUNT NUMBER _____

                                Signature _____

Rhine Bank   Address _____
South Street, Philadelphia, Pennsylvania 19104   _____

---

2. How would you change the withdrawal slip if you wanted to receive your money in the form of a check instead of in cash? Explain.

_____

_____

3. Suppose you needed to withdraw $2,000 from your account. Would you get the money in a check or in cash? Explain.

_____

_____

MAINTAINING SKILLS

Compute.

1. $51.61
    $\times$ 8

2. $3\overline{)\$180.93}$

3. $67.00
   − 25.60

4. $75.21
   + 21.35

Pacemaker ® Practical Mathematics for Consumers© Pearson Education, Inc. / Globe Fearon / Pearson Learning Group. All rights reserved.

Name _____   Date _____

Lesson 6.4

You must write a check to the Northeast Cable Company to pay this month's cable bill. The bill is $39.95.

```
                                              16-66
                                              1220         NO. 243

                          DATE _____

PAY TO THE
ORDER OF _____  $ [        ]

_____  DOLLARS

Smith Bank
1002 Sixth Avenue
New York, NY 10012

MEMO_____    _____

  ⑆1220 0667⑆  876305519⑈
```

Use the information above to complete Exercises 1–4.

1. Fill in your personal information on the check above. Then write the check to pay the cable bill this month.

2. What is the check number? _____

3. What is the account number? _____

4. What did you write on the memo line? Why? _____

_____

MAINTAINING SKILLS

Write each of these amounts in words as if you were writing a check.

1. $18.67 _____

2. $61.20 _____

3. $1,000.00 _____

4. $2,345.68 _____

Pacemaker ® Practical Mathematics for Consumers© Pearson Education, Inc. / Globe Fearon / Pearson Learning Group. All rights reserved.

Name _____ Date _____

Lessons 6.5 and 6.6

This is Norman's check register for part of January.

		PLEASE BE SURE TO DEDUCT ANY CHECK CHARGES THAT MAY APPLY TO YOUR ACCOUNT					BALANCE	
NUMBER	DATE	DESCRIPTION OF TRANSACTION	(−) CHECK/DEBIT	✔	(+) DEPOSIT	$	1,037	21
109	1/14	Del Cable	49	37				
		cable bill						
	1/16	Groceries R Us	102	59				
		Groceries						
	1/17	Deposit			298	31		
		Paycheck						
	1/19	ATM withdrawal	161	50				
		(+ $1.50 fee)						
110	1/20	Northern Realty	450	00				
		Rent						

Use the information above to solve each problem. Show your work.

1. What is the beginning balance of Norman's account? _____

2. What is the balance on each of the five dates? Write your answers in the check register.

3. What is the number of the check Norman wrote to pay his cable bill? _____

4. What is the amount of the fee Norman was charged to make a withdrawal from an ATM? _____

5. On which date did Norman use his debit card to make a purchase? _____

MAINTAINING SKILLS

Compute.

1. $16.47
   × 5

2. 4)$156.76

3. $2,987.66
   − 456.42

4. $41.78
   × 12

5. $30.50 × 0.7 = _____

6. $16.25 + $15.24 + $29.78 = _____

Pacemaker ® Practical Mathematics for Consumers© Pearson Education, Inc. / Globe Fearon / Pearson Learning Group. All rights reserved.

Name _____ Date _____

Lesson 6.7

Gina's bank statement and check register are below. They need to be reconciled.

Gina Baker						
87 Winding Way				Closing Date: 10/28/03		
Las Vegas, NV 89125				Beginning Balance: $345.62		

CHECKS

Check Number	Date Paid	Amount		Check Number	Date Paid	Amount
107	9/29/02	74.61		109*	10/28/03	102.38

OTHER CHARGES

	Date	Amount
Service Charge	10/1/03	6.00

DEPOSITS

Date	Amount		Date	Amount
10/9/03	322.33		10/26/03	38.92

Ending Balance: $523.88

		PLEASE BE SURE TO DEDUCT ANY CHECK CHARGES THAT MAY APPLY TO YOUR ACCOUNT						BALANCE	
NUMBER	DATE	DESCRIPTION OF TRANSACTION	(−) CHECK/DEBIT		✔	(+) DEPOSIT		$ 345	62
107	9/27	Toy Craze	74	61				271	01
	10/9	Deposit				322	33	593	34
108	10/25	Super Foods	121	50				471	84
	10/26	Deposit				38	92	510	76
109	10/26	Dainty Desserts	102	38				408	38

Use the information above to complete Exercises 1–3.

1. What is the closing date on the bank statement? _____

2. List the numbers of any outstanding checks. _____

3. What charge did Gina forget to include in her check register? _____

MAINTAINING SKILLS

Multiply or divide.

1. $24.10 × 0.8   2. $45.55 × 18   3. $5\overline{)\$23.25}$ 4. $74.15 ÷ 0.5

Pacemaker ® Practical Mathematics for Consumers© Pearson Education, Inc. / Globe Fearon / Pearson Learning Group. All rights reserved.

Name _____ Date _____

Lesson 6.8

The balance on your bank statement does not match the balance in your check register. You need to reconcile your account.

Wise Bank • Reconciliation Statement	
BALANCE SHOWN ON BANK STATEMENT $ 628.80	**BALANCE SHOWN IN CHECK REGISTER** $ 746.75

Wise Bank • Reconciliation Statement

BALANCE SHOWN ON BANK STATEMENT $ 628.80

PLUS: Deposits in Transit

① | Date | Amount |
|---|---|
| | |
| | |

| Total Deposits in Transit | |
| Subtotal | |

LESS: Checks Outstanding

Number	Amount

| Total Checks Outstanding | |

ADJUSTED BANK BALANCE
② $ _____

BALANCE SHOWN IN CHECK REGISTER $ 746.75

PLUS: Corrections

Description	Amount

| Total Additions | |
| Subtotal | |

LESS: Fees and Corrections

③ | Description | Amount |
|---|---|
| | |

| Total Deductions | |

ADJUSTED CHECKBOOK BALANCE
④ $ _____

Answer each question. Use the reconciliation statement above.

1. You deposited two checks today. One check was for $60.25, the other check was for $10.70. Record these transactions in the reconciliation statement.

2. What is your adjusted bank balance?

3. You forgot to record a $7 service charge and a $40 ATM withdrawal in your check register. Write these transactions in the statement.

4. What is your adjusted checkbook balance?

5. Is your account balanced now? Explain. _____

_____

MAINTAINING SKILLS

Add or subtract.

1.	$12.25	**2.**	$61.08	**3.**	$93.75	**4.**	$77.77
	+ 13.16		+ 9.28		− 29.36		− 15.17

Pacemaker ® Practical Mathematics for Consumers® Pearson Education, Inc. / Globe Fearon / Pearson Learning Group. All rights reserved.

7 ▷ Do You Want a Credit Card?

Exercise 30

Lesson 7.1

Write *T* next to each statement that is true. Write *F* next to each statement that is false. If the statement is false, rewrite it to make it true.

_____ **1.** A credit card lets you buy something now and pay later.

_____ **2.** You must pay at least the minimum payment on your credit card by the due date.

_____ **3.** If you pay the entire balance on your credit card every month, you will not owe any interest.

_____ **4.** The balance on your credit card is $78. You pay $60. Your unpaid balance is now $22.

Answer each question.

5. List three good things about credit cards.

 • _____

 • _____

 • _____

6. List three bad things about credit cards.

 • _____

 • _____

 • _____

MAINTAINING SKILLS

Compute.

1. $436.78
     + 517.01

2. $98.65
     − 9.58

3. $112.40
     + 43.15

4. $145.67
       26.32
     + 18.98

5. $591 ÷ 10 = _____

6. $300 × 15 = _____

Pacemaker ® Practical Mathematics for Consumers© Pearson Education, Inc. / Globe Fearon / Pearson Learning Group. All rights reserved.

Name _____ Date _____

Lesson 7.2

Fill in the credit card application below.

Credit Card Application

Please print and provide all requested information below.

FIRST NAME	INITIAL	LAST NAME

/ /	— —		
DATE OF BIRTH	SOCIAL SECURITY NUMBER	DRIVER'S LICENSE NUMBER	STATE

MOTHER'S MAIDEN NAME	☐ RENT ☐ OWN	HOW LONG? [ ] YRS. [ ] MOS.	HOME PHONE ([ ]) [—]

	APT#	CITY	STATE	ZIP
CURRENT HOME ADDRESS				

	APT#	CITY	STATE	ZIP
PREVIOUS HOME ADDRESS (If less than 2 years at current address)				

		YRS. MOS.
EMPLOYER NAME	POSITION	HOW LONG?

	([ ]) [—]
BUSINESS ADDRESS	BUSINESS PHONE

FORMER EMPLOYER (If less than 2 years at current employer)

TYPE OF ACCOUNT REQUESTED (CHECK ONE):   ☐ INDIVIDUAL   ☐ JOINT

CO-APPLICANT INFORMATION (if Joint Account requested)

FIRST NAME	INITIAL	LAST NAME

RELATIONSHIP TO APPLICANT (if any)	SOCIAL SECURITY NUMBER — —

		YRS. MOS.
EMPLOYER NAME	POSITION	HOW LONG?

	([ ]) [—]	([ ]) [—]
EMPLOYER ADDRESS	BUSINESS PHONE	HOME PHONE

BANK—LIST BRANCH AND ADDRESS	☐ CHECKING ☐ SAVINGS

MAINTAINING SKILLS

Divide. Round to the nearest cent if necessary.

1. $15\overline{)\$659}$ **2.** $6\overline{)\$259}$ **3.** $10\overline{)\$78}$ **4.** $3\overline{)\$157}$

Pacemaker ® Practical Mathematics for Consumers© Pearson Education, Inc. / Globe Fearon / Pearson Learning Group. All rights reserved.

Name _____ Date _____

7 ▷ How Do You Protect Your Credit Card?　　Exercise 32

Lesson 7.3

Answer each question.

1. The credit card Janice applied for just arrived in the mail. What should she do first?

2. Noelle's credit card was stolen and $1,000 worth of items were charged to her card. Noelle immediately reported the card stolen. What is the most she will have to pay?

3. Someone Mark did not know called Mark on the telephone and asked for his credit card number. Mark gave his credit card information to the caller. Why was this a bad idea? Explain.

   _____

   _____

4. List two reasons why you should not let anyone use your credit card.

   • _____

   • _____

5. Why should you keep your credit card receipts? Explain.

   _____

   _____

MAINTAINING SKILLS

Find each percent.

1. $25 out of $100 _____　　2. $8 out of $64 _____

3. $248 out of $400 _____　　4. $522 out of $600 _____

Pacemaker ® Practical Mathematics for Consumers© Pearson Education, Inc. / Globe Fearon / Pearson Learning Group. All rights reserved.

Name _____ Date _____

Pacemaker ® Practical Mathematics for Consumers© Pearson Education, Inc. / Globe Fearon / Pearson Learning Group. All rights reserved.

7 ▶ What About Buying on Credit?   Exercise 33

Lesson 7.4

 Find each monthly percentage rate. Then calculate the finance charge for one month on the unpaid balance.

	Name	Unpaid Balance	Annual Percentage Rate	Monthly Percentage Rate	Finance Charge
1.	Tamir	$250	18%		
2.	Cecilia	$400	15%		
3.	Dennis	$730	18%		
4.	Annette	$620	12%		
5.	Kenny	$842	24%		

Solve each problem.

6. Edmund's credit card has an unpaid balance of $598. The annual percentage rate is 18%. What will be the finance charge for one month on this amount?

7. Tori had a $300 unpaid balance after last month's payment on her account. Her annual percentage rate is 21%. The minimum payment due is $25. How much of that is interest for one month on the unpaid balance?

MAINTAINING SKILLS

Compute.

1. $57.21
   + 7.20

2. 2)10.7

3.   125
   × 0.3

4. $38.00
   − 24.10

5. $15.50 ÷ 5 = _____

6. $102.54 + $64.32 = _____

Name _____ Date _____

Lesson 7.5

Use Jason's monthly statement to answer each question.

PAYMENT DUE DATE	YOUR NEW BALANCE	MINIMUM PAYMENT DUE	ENTER AMOUNT OF PAYMENT ENCLOSED
9/17/03	$239.10	$15	$ ☐☐☐,☐☐☐.☐☐

ACCOUNT NUMBER: 123-45-670

STATEMENT CLOSING DATE	DAYS IN BILLING CYCLE
08/22/03	31

CREDIT LIMIT	AVAILABLE CREDIT	CASH ADVANCE LIMIT	AVAILABLE CREDIT FOR CASH ADVANCE
$1,500.00	$1,260.90	$500.00	$500.00

CHARGES AND CREDITS

Activity Date	Post Date	Reference Number	Activity	Amount
08/12	08/12		Payment	−25.00
08/15	08/15	SJH6	Pets and More	+39.50
08/17	08/18	8RT7	Super D Groceries	+65.72

For Finance Charge

	Annual Percentage Rate
Purchases	18.0%
Cash Advances	19.0%

ACCOUNT SUMMARY:

Previous Balance	Total
	$156.53
(−) Payments, Credits	− 25.00
(+) Purchases, Cash, Debits	+ 105.22
(+) FINANCE CHARGES	+ 2.35
(=) New Balance	$239.10
Minimum Payment Due	$15.00

For answers to any questions, please call us at 1-888-555-1234.

1. How much is Jason's minimum payment?

2. Can Jason buy new furniture that costs $1,700 with his credit card account? Explain. _____

_____

MAINTAINING SKILLS

Write each decimal as a percent.

1. 0.05 _____ **2.** 0.67 _____ **3.** 0.845 _____ **4.** 1.25 _____

Pacemaker ® Practical Mathematics for Consumers© Pearson Education, Inc. / Globe Fearon / Pearson Learning Group. All rights reserved.

7 ▶ **What Happens When You Return an Item?** Exercise 35

Lesson 7.6

Find each new balance.

	Previous Balance	New Purchases	Finance Charge	Credits	Payment	New Balance
1.	$43	$107	$1.20	$42	$20	
2.	$200	$61	$6.10	$127	$100	
3.	$130	$310	$4.00	none	$60	
4.	$85	$200	$3.90	$94	$50	
5.	$400	$420	$7.60	$150	$40	

Solve each problem. Show your work.

6. Erica used her credit card to pay the $275 repair bill for her car. She also returned a sweater and a shirt for $68. Erica had a previous balance of $50 and a finance charge of $0.92. What will be the new balance on her statement?

7. Chip used his credit card to buy work tools. He spent $125. He returned one tool for $36. He had a previous balance of $212 and a finance charge of $4.30. This month Chip will pay $130. What will be the new balance on his statement?

MAINTAINING SKILLS

Write each percent as a decimal.

1. 2.4% _____   **2.** 81% _____   **3.** 9.9% _____   **4.** 64% _____

Pacemaker ® Practical Mathematics for Consumers© Pearson Education, Inc. / Globe Fearon / Pearson Learning Group. All rights reserved.

Name _____ Date _____

Lesson 7.7

Find each percent of take-home pay. Then decide if buying
on credit is a good idea for each person. Write *yes* or *no*.
(Hint: Payments should be no more than 20% of take-home pay.)

	Name	Total Monthly Credit Card Payments	Monthly Take-home Pay	Percent of Take-home Pay	Is this person buying too much on credit?
1.	Corey	$120	$1,250		
2.	Luz	$205	$1,000		
3.	Pedro	$300	$1,500		
4.	Mike	$180	$1,000		
5.	Claudia	$95	$1,900		

Solve each problem. Show your work.

6. Maureen's monthly take-home pay is $1,000. Her credit card
payments are usually $120 a month. She plans to buy a new
refrigerator. This will increase her monthly credit card payments
to $160. Should Maureen use her credit card to pay for the
refrigerator? Explain.

_____

_____

7. Jasper's weekly take-home pay is $345. What is the most he
should be paying each month on credit cards each month?

MAINTAINING SKILLS

Write each decimal as a percent.

1. 0.48 _____   **2.** 0.361 _____   **3.** 0.25 _____   **4.** 0.525 _____

Pacemaker ® Practical Mathematics for Consumers© Pearson Education, Inc. / Globe Fearon / Pearson Learning Group. All rights reserved.

Name _____ Date _____

Lesson 7.8

 **Solve each problem. Show your work.
Use a calculator if you like.**

1. Paul gets a $360 cash advance on his credit card. The annual
   percentage rate on a cash advance is 24%. What is the finance
   charge on the cash advance for one month?

2. The annual percentage rate on a cash advance is 26%. The APR
   on a credit card purchase is 14%. How much more interest do
   you pay in one month on a $600 cash advance compared to
   a $600 purchase?

**Find the total finance charge for the month. (Hint: First find the
finance charge for the cash advance. Then find the finance charge
for the purchase. Then add.)**

	Cash Advance	Cash Advance APR	Amount of Purchase	Purchase APR	Total Finance Charge
3.	$300	24%	$0	18%	
4.	$400	15%	$95	10%	
5.	$600	18%	$140	15%	
6.	$400	18%	$210	12%	
7.	$800	24%	$300	24%	

MAINTAINING SKILLS

Subtract.

1. $100.32
    −   54.25

2. $47.25
    − 22.08

3. $156.32
    − 132.60

4. $64.20
    − 51.03

Pacemaker ® Practical Mathematics for Consumers© Pearson Education, Inc. / Globe Fearon / Pearson Learning Group. All rights reserved.

Name _____ Date _____

Lessons 8.1 and 8.2

Answer each question. Show your work.

1. Darius wants a car loan. He has worked at the same job for three years. He has lived in his own apartment for two and a half years and he always pays his rent and bills on time. Do you think the bank should give Darius a loan? Explain.

_____

_____

2. Which of the following might make it harder for you to get a loan to buy a house? Circle the letter of the correct answer.

A. having a savings account

B. paying your bills on time

C. having a lien on your car

D. working at a steady job

3. Saul needs a student loan for computer school. He compares the rates on two loans. Bank A offers a 10.25% interest rate on the loan. Bank B offers a 10.50% interest rate on the loan. If all other terms and conditions are the same, where should Saul apply for the loan? Explain.

_____

_____

4. A new car loan has a term of loan from 2–6 years and the interest rate is between 4% and 8%. What is the longest amount of time you could take to pay off the car loan? What is the best interest rate you could get?

MAINTAINING SKILLS

Find the percent of each number.

1. 10% of 45 _____

2. 15% of 700 _____

3. 54% of 39 _____

4. 35% of 110 _____

Pacemaker ® Practical Mathematics for Consumers© Pearson Education, Inc. / Globe Fearon / Pearson Learning Group. All rights reserved.

Name _____ Date _____

Lesson 8.3

 Find the simple interest on each loan. Then find the total amount that will be paid on each loan.

	Principal	Interest Rate	Term of the Loan	Interest	Total Amount Paid
1.	$1,700	18%	1 year		
2.	$4,300	17%	2 years		
3.	$6,100	16.5%	3 years		
4.	$3,200	20%	4 years		

 Find the number of monthly payments for each loan. Then find the monthly payment. Round to the nearest cent.

	Total Amount Paid	Term of the Loan	Number of Monthly Payments	Monthly Payment
5.	$1,150	1 year		
6.	$3,100	3 years		
7.	$4,250	4 years		
8.	$5,790	2 years		

MAINTAINING SKILLS

Add.

1. $123.65
       22.57
   + 39.12

2. $12.25
      14.52
   + 9.31

3. $987.35
   + 45.67

4.   542
     61
   + 13

5.   12.4 + 5.2 + 15.6 = _____

6.   176 + 298 + 155 = _____

Pacemaker ® Practical Mathematics for Consumers© Pearson Education, Inc. / Globe Fearon / Pearson Learning Group. All rights reserved.

8 ▸ What Is on a Loan Application?   Exercise 40

Lesson 8.4

Fill out the loan application below.

You want to buy a used car for $1,000. You decide to apply for
a one-year loan. You earn $24,000 a year.

SECTION A: YOUR CREDIT REQUEST

WHAT DO YOU WANT THIS LOAN FOR?_____

LOAN $ _____ FOR ___ MONTHS ☐ FIXED INTEREST RATE   (Explain Purpose)

THIS APPLICATION IS ☐ IN YOUR NAME ALONE ☐ JOINTLY WITH _____
If applying jointly, each of you must complete a separate application.

SECTION B: YOURSELF

FIRST NAME   MIDDLE INITIAL   LAST NAME

CURRENT ADDRESS   STREET   APT. NO.   TIME THERE
                                                            YRS.   MOS.

CITY   STATE   ZIP CODE   ☐ OWN ☐ RENT

PREVIOUS ADDRESS   STREET   APT. NO.   TIME THERE
(If at current address less than three years)   YRS.   MOS.

CITY   STATE   ZIP CODE   DATE OF BIRTH

SOCIAL SECURITY NO.   DRIVER'S LICENSE NO.

HOME PHONE NO.   DEPENDENTS OTHER THAN SELF OR SPOUSE

BEST TIME TO CALL YOU   BEST PLACE TO CALL YOU
☐ MORNING ☐ AFTERNOON ☐ EVENING   ☐ HOME ☐ WORK

MARITAL STATUS ☐ MARRIED   ☐ SINGLE ☐ SEPARATED ☐ DIVORCED

SECTION C: YOUR INCOME

MONTHLY GROSS SALARY/WAGES	$
DIVIDENDS AND INTEREST	$
OTHER INCOME (DESCRIBE)	$
YOUR TOTAL MONTHLY INCOME	$

MAINTAINING SKILLS

Subtract.

1. $57.87
    − 42.36

2. $895.21
    − 438.16

3. $124.25
    − 67.85

4. $12.34 − $7.21 = _____

Pacemaker ® Practical Mathematics for Consumers© Pearson Education, Inc. / Globe Fearon / Pearson Learning Group. All rights reserved.

8 ▶ **What Is the Fee on a Loan?**   **Exercise 41**

Lesson 8.5

Solve each problem. Show your work.

	Amount of Loan	Deducted Fee	Amount Left
1.	$700	$60	
2.	$1,100	$100	
3.	$1,900	$150	
4.	$2,700	$175	
5.	$4,500	5%	
6.	$5,000	6%	
7.	$950	$55	

8. Jordan took out a loan for $1,600. The fee was 3% of the loan. The fee was deducted from the loan. How much of the loan was left?

9. Clarissa took out a loan for $3,800. The fee was 6% of the loan. The fee was deducted from the loan. How much was the fee? How much of the loan was left?

10. Candy took out a loan for $2,450. The fee was 2.5% of the loan. How much was the fee?

MAINTAINING SKILLS

Divide to find the percent.

1. $\frac{27}{90}$ 2. $\frac{18}{36}$ 3. $\frac{90}{1,000}$ 4. $\frac{5}{100}$

Pacemaker ® Practical Mathematics for Consumers© Pearson Education, Inc. / Globe Fearon / Pearson Learning Group. All rights reserved.

9 ▸ How Much Can You Afford for Rent?   Exercise 42

Lesson 9.1

Complete the chart. Each person spends 25% of his or her monthly income on rent. (Hint: For Exercises 3–5, first find the monthly income.)

	Name	Income	Monthly Rent
1.	Ann	$1,600 per month	
2.	Justine	$2,200 per month	
3.	Bonnie	$250 per week	
4.	Jason	$26,880 per year	
5.	James	$18,000 per year	

Solve each problem. Show your work.

6. Stephanie's hourly wage is $16. She works 40 hours a week. What is her weekly income? What is her monthly income? She pays 30% of her income for rent every month, what does she pay?

_____

7. Chris found an apartment for $750 a month. The most he can spend on rent is 30% of his monthly income. His monthly income is $2,300. Can he afford the apartment? Explain.

_____

_____

_____

MAINTAINING SKILLS

Find each percent.

1. 40% of $5,600 _____   2. 15% of $580 _____

3. 20% of $872 _____   4. 35% of $750 _____

Pacemaker ® Practical Mathematics for Consumers© Pearson Education, Inc. / Globe Fearon / Pearson Learning Group. All rights reserved.

Name _____ Date _____

 9 ▶ **How Do You Find the Place You Need?** **Exercise 43**

Lesson 9.2

Solve each problem. Use the classified ads below. Show your work.

| **Pebble Dr.**—2 BR, washer/dryer in basement, close to train, no pets allowed. $690/mo | **Boulder Ave.**—2BR, EIK, hwd flrs, pets allowed, $620/mo | **Stone Pl.**—Studio, heat & hot water incl., close to train, $450/mo | **Rock Rd.**—1BR, walk up to 4th fl, pets allowed, hwd flrs, AC, $550/mo |

1. Mary needs an apartment immediately that will allow pets. Her weekly income is $570. She cannot spend more than 25% of her monthly income on rent. Which apartment should she choose?

2. Lou is looking for an apartment. He can afford to spend $550 a month. He wants heat and hot water included in the monthly rent. Which apartment should he choose?

3. Carol and her friend decide to rent the apartment on Boulder Avenue. They will split the rent equally. How much will they each pay for rent?

4. Stacey earns $2,400 a month. She can afford to spend 25% of her monthly income on rent. Which apartments can she afford?

MAINTAINING SKILLS

Change each percent to a decimal.

1. 30% _____
2. 12% _____
3. 50% _____
4. 3.7% _____

Pacemaker ® Practical Mathematics for Consumers© Pearson Education, Inc. / Globe Fearon / Pearson Learning Group. All rights reserved.

9 ▶ What Is in a Lease?   Exercise 44

Lesson 9.3

Solve each problem. Show your work.

1. Lynn signed a one-year lease. She pays $600 per month in rent. If she wants to move out 2 months early, how much money will she owe when she moves out?

2. Kashif pays $520 per month in rent. He signed a one-year lease beginning on October 1. He decided to move out at the end of May. How much money does Kashif owe when he moves out?

3. Carla pays $690 a month in rent. She signed an 18-month lease. If she moves out after 1 year, how much money will she owe?

4. Daniel shares an apartment. He and his roomate have a one-year lease. They each pay $320 a month in rent. If Daniel moves out 2 months early, how much money does he need to pay?

MAINTAINING SKILLS

Compute.

1. $104.57
    $\times \quad 13$

2. $19.11
    $+ 11.25$

3. $115.00
    $- \quad 20.01$

4. $12\overline{)\$180}$

5. $125 ÷ 10 = $ _____

6. $15.23 + $6.25 + $135.67 = $ _____

Pacemaker ® Practical Mathematics for Consumers© Pearson Education, Inc. / Globe Fearon / Pearson Learning Group. All rights reserved.

Name _____ Date _____

Lesson 9.4

Solve each problem. Show your work.

1. Felicia found an apartment that rents for $470 a month. The landlord requires one and a half month's rent for the security deposit and the first month's rent before Felicia can move in. How much does Felicia pay altogether before she can move into her new apartment?

2. Kevin moved out of his apartment. The hardwood floors in Kevin's apartment were damaged. The landlord paid $800 to replace part of the floor. Kevin had paid $1,140 as a security deposit. How much did he get back when he moved out?

3. You and a friend find an apartment you both like. The rent is $940 a month and you must give a security deposit equal to one and a half month's rent. The first month's rent and the security deposit are due before you can move into your new apartment. They will be divided equally. How much will you each pay before you can move in?

4. Christine has $3,000 in her savings account. She found an apartment she likes that rents for $425 a month. The landlord requires two month's rent for the security deposit and the first month's rent before Christine can move in. How much will Christine have left in her savings account after she gives the landlord the security deposit and pays the rent?

MAINTAINING SKILLS

Write each as a percent. Round to the nearest whole percent.

1. $16 out of $100 _____ 2. $45 out of $90 _____ 3. $245 out of $600 _____

Pacemaker ® Practical Mathematics for Consumers© Pearson Education, Inc. / Globe Fearon / Pearson Learning Group. All rights reserved.

9 ▸ Can You Afford to Buy a House?   Exercise 46

Lesson 9.5

Find the amount of money each person can afford to borrow. (Hint: Use the banker's rule.)

	Name	Annual Income	Amount That Can Be Borrowed
1.	Luke	$25,200	
2.	Emril	$29,850	
3.	Selina	$35,100	
4.	Hassan	$27,000	
5.	Neil	$21,900	

Solve each problem. Show your work.

6. Anthony found a house he likes. He needs to borrow $62,000 to buy the house. What annual income does Anthony need in order to afford to borrow the money?

7. Kwon found a house he likes. He needs to borrow $84,000 to buy the house. What annual income does Kwon need in order to afford to borrow the money?

8. Jessica earns $2,840 a month. Can she afford to borrow $90,000 to buy the house she likes? Explain.

_____

_____

MAINTAINING SKILLS

Divide.

1. 3)$63.27

2. 4)$250

3. $160 ÷ 4 _____

4. $98 ÷ 2.5 _____

Pacemaker ® Practical Mathematics for Consumers© Pearson Education, Inc. / Globe Fearon / Pearson Learning Group. All rights reserved.

9 ▶ **How Much Is the Down Payment?**   **Exercise 47**

Lesson 9.6

Solve each problem. Show your work.

1. Evan found a house for $109,000. He needs a 20% down payment.
    How much money does Evan need for the down payment?

2. Tania found a house for $96,000. She will pay 5% of the price of
    the house as a down payment. How much will the mortgage be?

3. Stuart found a house for $117,000. He will pay 15% of the price of
    the house as a down payment. How much will the mortgage be?

Find each down payment and mortgage.

	Name	Price of House	Rate of Down Payment	Down Payment	Mortgage
4.	Kristi	$105,200	5%		
5.	Antonio	$142,000	3%		
6.	Najeem	$170,000	20%		
7.	Helen	$114,200	15%		
8.	Ramona	$99,000	10%		

MAINTAINING SKILLS

Multiply.

1. $25.05
    × 16

2. $52.50
    × 4.2

3. $42.15
    × 0.2

4. $115.50
    × 1.5

Pacemaker ® Practical Mathematics for Consumers© Pearson Education, Inc. / Globe Fearon / Pearson Learning Group. All rights reserved.

Name _____ Date _____

9 ▸ How Much is the Monthly Mortgage Payment?

Exercise 48

Lesson 9.7

 Solve each problem. Use the chart below. Show your work.

Monthly Payments for Fixed-Rate 30-Year Mortgage								
Mortgage Amount	Interest Rate							
	6%	6.5%	7%	7.5%	8%	8.5%	9%	10%
$40,000	$246	$252	$266	$280	$294	$308	$322	$351
$50,000	308	316	333	350	367	385	402	439
$60,000	369	379	399	420	440	461	483	527
$70,000	431	442	466	489	514	538	563	614
$80,000	493	506	532	559	587	615	644	702
$90,000	554	569	599	629	660	692	724	790
$100,000	616	632	665	699	734	768	805	878

1. Jared took out a 30-year mortgage for $50,000 at 6.5%. How much is his monthly mortgage payment?

2. Jocelyn took out a 30-year mortgage for $100,000 at 8.5%. How much is her monthly mortgage payment?

3. Irene took out a 30-year mortgage for $90,000 at 7.5%. How much will she pay over one year?

4. Ed took out a 30-year mortgage for $60,000 at 10%. How much interest will he pay over 30 years? (Hint: First find how much he will pay in total over 30 years. Then subtract the amount of the mortgage.)

MAINTAINING SKILLS

Add.

1. $78.99
      + 1.25

2. $19.25
      + 37.36

3. $57.20
      + 2.50

4. $44.59
      + 80.52

Pacemaker ® Practical Mathematics for Consumers© Pearson Education, Inc. / Globe Fearon / Pearson Learning Group. All rights reserved.

9 ▶ What About Closing Costs?   Exercise 49

Lesson 9.8

Solve each problem. Show your work.

1. Noah's closing costs are 4% of the price of the house. His new house costs $97,500. How much will Noah have to pay for closing costs?

2. Clara's closing costs are 3% of the price of the house. Her new house costs $102,000. Her mother will give her $2,000 toward the closing costs. How much more money will Clara need to cover the closing costs?

3. Vincent is buying a house for $135,000. He wants to know how much his closing costs will be. What is the maximum amount Vincent will need for closing costs? (Hint: The maximum amount is 6% of the price of the house.)

4. Amber's closing costs are 3.5% of the price of the house. The house costs $86,000. How much will Amber have to pay for closing costs?

5. Seth found a house he would like to buy. The house costs $122,000. He has $8,000 set aside for closing costs. Assuming closing costs are no more than 6% of the price of the house, will he have enough money to pay the closing costs? Explain.

_____

_____

_____

MAINTAINING SKILLS

Write each fraction as a decimal.

1. $\frac{2}{10}$

2. $\frac{70}{1,000}$

3. $\frac{16}{20}$

4. $\frac{45}{100}$

5. $\frac{27}{108}$

6. $\frac{6}{120}$

Pacemaker ® Practical Mathematics for Consumers© Pearson Education, Inc. / Globe Fearon / Pearson Learning Group. All rights reserved.

Name _____ Date _____

Lesson 9.9

Each person in the chart below makes a monthly real estate
tax payment with the mortgage payment. Complete the chart.

	Name	Annual Real Estate Tax	Monthly Real Estate Tax	Monthly Mortgage Payment	Monthly Bank Payment
1.	Rasheen	$1,200		$750	
2.	Camille	$780		$460	
3.	Jake	$1,440		$660	

Solve each problem. Show your work. Round to the nearest cent.

4. Jamal pays $1,768 a year for real estate tax on his house. He makes a
   real estate tax payment each month. How much does he pay each
   month for real estate tax?

5. Isabella pays $2,210 a year for real estate tax on her house. She makes
   a real estate tax payment each quarter. How much does she pay each
   quarter for real estate tax?

6. Jimmy pays $3,828 a year for real estate tax on his house. He sends a
   real estate tax payment each month to the bank with his mortgage
   payment. His mortgage payment is $685 a month. How much does he
   pay the bank altogether each month?

MAINTAINING SKILLS

Add.

1.	$625.50 + 110.75	**2.**	$1,016.00 + 722.91	**3.**	$25.25 + 15.20	**4.**	$11.09 + 1.81

Pacemaker ® Practical Mathematics for Consumers© Pearson Education, Inc. / Globe Fearon / Pearson Learning Group. All rights reserved.

Name _____ Date _____

 9 ▶ **What About Homeowner's Insurance?** **Exercise 51**

Lesson 9.10

Solve each problem. Show your work.

1. Gary buys a house. Homeowner's insurance will cost $860 a year. He needs to pay 20% of this amount as his first payment. How much is his first payment?

2. Becky buys a house. Homeowner's insurance will cost $710 a year. She needs to pay 25% of this amount as her first payment. How much is her first payment?

3. Erma buys a house. Homeowner's insurance will cost $595 a year. She needs to pay 15% of this amount as her first payment. How much is her first payment? What is her balance after she makes the first payment?

4. Rob's homeowner's insurance costs $600 a year. His first payment is $120. Then each payment is 10% of what he owes after the first payment. How much is each remaining payment?

5. Marie's homeowner's insurance costs $539 a year. Her first payment is $134.75. Then each additional payment is 12% of what she owes after the first payment. How much is each remaining payment?

MAINTAINING SKILLS

Compute.

1. $569 − $112 = _____

2. 7)$422.10

3. $903 + $42 + $26.54 = _____

4. $912 + $32.90 = _____

5. 2.5)$448

6. $200 × 0.15 = _____

Pacemaker ® Practical Mathematics for Consumers© Pearson Education, Inc. / Globe Fearon / Pearson Learning Group. All rights reserved.

10 How Can You Furnish Your Home on a Limited Budget?

Lessons 10.1 and 10.2

Sheila made a list of items she needs to buy for her new apartment. The items are listed in order of priority. Use Sheila's list to answer Questions 1 and 2.

THINGS TO BUY
1. Table and chairs
2. Sofa
3. Coffee table
4. Dresser
5. TV
6. CD Player

1. Which item is Sheila's highest priority?

2. Sheila has $150 to spend on items for her apartment. She found a table and chair set for $110. She also found a TV for $120 and a CD player for $100. Based on her list, which of the items should Sheila buy? Explain.

_____

_____

_____

Solve each problem. Show your work.

3. You see a classified ad for a sofa and coffee table for $120. You offer the seller $80. He rejects your offer but agrees to lower the price by $30. How much will you pay for the items?

4. You have $250 to furnish your new apartment. You go to a used furniture store and buy a kitchen table and chairs for $110, two chairs for the living room for $24 each, a coffee table for $30, and a dresser for $59. How much money will you have left?

MAINTAINING SKILLS

Subtract.

1.	$10.00	2.	$24.34	3.	$125.68	4.	$96.31
	− 3.83		− 9.80		− 54.13		− 74.01

Pacemaker ® Practical Mathematics for Consumers© Pearson Education, Inc. / Globe Fearon / Pearson Learning Group. All rights reserved.

10 ▶ Should You Buy on Sale?   Exercise 53

Lesson 10.3

Solve each problem. Show your work. Round to the nearest cent if necessary.

1. Amir needs to buy a new toaster. The original price of the toaster is $24.99. It is on sale for 10% off. How much will Amir pay for the toaster on sale?

2. Lamont needs a new comforter for his bed. The original price of the one he likes is $59.99. All comforters are on sale for 15% off. He has a coupon for an additional 10% off the sale price. How much will Lamont save on the comforter?

3. Marcia needs a new shower curtain and four bath towels. The shower curtain costs $17.99. Each bath towel costs $9.99. Marcia has a coupon. If she spends $50 she will get $10 off. What will her total be for the shower curtain and bath towels?

4. Lillian needs a new vacuum. She finds one for $149.99 on sale for 30% off. She applies for the store's credit card so she will get an additional 15% off the sale price. How much will the vacuum cost? How much will Lillian save?

MAINTAINING SKILLS

Find the percent of each number.

1. 17% of $112 _____ **2.** 2.5% of $98 _____ **3.** 46% of $357 _____

4. 3% of $987 _____ **5.** 2% of $25 _____ **6.** 14% of $57 _____

Pacemaker ® Practical Mathematics for Consumers© Pearson Education, Inc. / Globe Fearon / Pearson Learning Group. All rights reserved.

Name _____ Date _____

Lesson 10.4

Use the energy guide on the right to solve each problem.

1. Suppose you kept this refrigerator for 15 years. What would your cost be to operate it over that length of time if the electricity cost per kilowatt-hour in your area is 4 cents?

2. Tania bought a new refrigerator. She lives in an area that charges 6 cents per kilowatt-hour of electricity. Tania's sister bought the same model refrigerator. She lives in an area that charges 10 cents per kilowatt-hour of electricity. How much more money will Tania's sister spend to operate her refrigerator for one year?

	Refrigerator-Freezer	**Model(s):** FR101, FR201, FR202
	Capacity: 24 Cubic Feet	**Type of Defrost:** Automatic

ENERGYGUIDE

Estimates on the scale based on a national average electric rate of 5¢ per kilowatt-hour.

Only models with 22.5 to 22.6 cubic feet are compared in the scale.

$91
THIS MODEL

Models with lowest energy cost
$70

Models with highest energy cost
$134

Estimated cost

Your cost will vary depending on your local energy rate and how you use the product.

How much will this model cost you to run yearly?

		Yearly Cost
		Estimated yearly cost shown below
Cost per kilowatt-hour	2¢	$37
	4¢	$74
	6¢	$110
	8¢	$146
	10¢	$183
	12¢	$219

Ask your salesperson or local utility for the energy rate (cost per kilowatt-hour) in your area.

Important: Removal of this label before consumer purchase is a violation of federal law (42 U.S.C. 6302).

MAINTAINING SKILLS

Add.

1. $8.36
   + 11.24

2. $199.23
   + 27.21

3. $13.45
   + 11.41

4. $29.98
   + 11.02

5. $41.20 + $29.70 + $1.30 = _____

6. $21.02 + $12.88 = _____

Pacemaker ® Practical Mathematics for Consumers© Pearson Education, Inc. / Globe Fearon / Pearson Learning Group. All rights reserved.

Name _____ Date _____

10 ▶ Which Plan Is Best for You?   Exercise 55

Lesson 10.5

Find the cost of each plan. Use the phone plan chart below.
Write your answers in the chart.

Phone Plans		
Charges	Plan A	Plan B
Monthly fee	None	$10.50
Price per minute weekdays	$0.17	Free first 75 minutes Then $0.05
Price per minute evenings/weekends	$0.08	Free first 150 minutes Then $0.02

	Name	Weekday Minutes Used	Evening/Weekend Minutes Used	Cost of Plan A	Cost of Plan B
1.	Davis	60	110		
2.	Ed	45	95		
3.	Sharon	110	180		
4.	Belle	70	160		
5.	Asa	95	200		

MAINTAINING SKILLS

Compute.

1. $\begin{array}{r} \$12 \\ \times\ 0.35 \\ \hline \end{array}$

2. $4\overline{)\$159}$

3. $\begin{array}{r} \$16.78 \\ 24.52 \\ +\ 17.89 \\ \hline \end{array}$

4. $168 \div 14 =$ _____

5. $\$25.36 \times 8.75 =$ _____

6. $\$258.36 - \$101.01 =$ _____

Pacemaker ® Practical Mathematics for Consumers© Pearson Education, Inc. / Globe Fearon / Pearson Learning Group. All rights reserved.

10 ► How Much Paint Will You Need?   **Exercise 56**

Lesson 10.7

Solve each problem. Show your work.

1. Zasha wants to paint her living room. The area to be painted is 300 square feet. One quart of paint covers 75 square feet. How many quarts of paint does she need?

2. Khalil wants to paint his kitchen. The area to be painted is 525 square feet. One quart of paint covers 90 square feet. How many quarts of paint does Khalil need?

3. Seung Min needs 3 gallons and 2 quarts of paint to paint his bedroom and hallway. A gallon of paint costs $14.99. A quart of paint costs $5.89. How much will it cost Seung Min to buy the paint for his bedroom and hallway?

4. Peter needs 5 gallons and 4 quarts of paint to paint some rooms in his house. A gallon of paint costs $13.89. A quart of paint costs $5.25. How much will it cost Peter to buy the paint for the rooms in his house? Would it be cheaper to buy 6 gallons of paint rather than 5 gallons and 4 quarts? Explain.

_____

_____

_____

MAINTAINING SKILLS

Find the average of each set of numbers.

1. $13, $25, $18, $10 _____   2. $21.50, $49.36, $38.25 _____

3. $98.36, $125.47, $37.89 _____   4. $61, $68, $97, $115, $81 _____

Pacemaker ® Practical Mathematics for Consumers© Pearson Education, Inc. / Globe Fearon / Pearson Learning Group. All rights reserved.

Name _____ Date _____

 10 **How Many Tiles Do You Need to Cover the Floor?**   Exercise 57

Lesson 10.8

Solve each problem. Show your work.

1. Marisol wants to put tile down on her bathroom floor. The floor is 8 feet long and 8 feet wide. Each tile covers 1 square foot. The tiles cost $1.45 each. What is the total cost of the tiles for Marisol's bathroom floor?

2. Yvonne wants to put tile down on her kitchen floor. The floor is 12 feet long and 10 feet wide. Each tile covers 1 square foot. The tiles cost $1.05 each. What is the total cost of the tiles for Yvonne's kitchen floor?

3. Jay wants to put tile down on his den floor. He needs 120 tiles. There are 25 tiles in a box. How many boxes of tile should John buy?

4. Will wants to put tile down on his hallway floor. The floor is 6 feet long by 4 feet wide. Each tile covers 1 square foot. There are 15 tiles in a box. Each box costs $15.75. How much will the tiles for Will's hallway floor cost?

MAINTAINING SKILLS

Write each percent as a decimal.

1. 8.5% _____   2. 16% _____   3. 3.7% _____

4. 1.9% _____   5. 12.7% _____   6. 2.1% _____

Pacemaker ® Practical Mathematics for Consumers© Pearson Education, Inc. / Globe Fearon / Pearson Learning Group. All rights reserved.

11 ▶ What Is a Balanced Diet?

Exercise 58

Lesson 11.1

Use the chart below to solve each problem.

Size of One Serving				
Milk Group	**Meat/Poultry/Fish Group**	**Vegetable Group**	**Fruit Group**	**Bread/Cereal Group**
1 cup of milk	2–3 ounces of cooked lean meat, poultry, or fish	1 cup of raw leafy vegetables	1 medium apple, banana, orange, or pear	1 slice of bread
1 cup of yogurt	1–1$\frac{1}{2}$ cups of cooked dry beans	$\frac{1}{2}$ cup of other vegetables — cooked or raw	$\frac{1}{2}$ cup of chopped, cooked, or canned fruit	1 cup of ready-to-eat cereal
1.5 ounces of natural cheese	2–3 eggs	$\frac{3}{4}$ cup of vegetable juice	$\frac{3}{4}$ cup of fruit juice	$\frac{1}{2}$ cup of rice

1. What is the size of 1 serving of canned fruit? _____

2. For dinner, Nick had 1 cup of rice, 1 cup of cooked carrots, 1 cup of cooked mushrooms, and 4 ounces of chicken. How

    many servings from each food group were in his dinner? _____

    _____

3. A balanced diet includes 2–3 servings from the milk group a day. Janice has a $\frac{1}{2}$ cup of milk with her cereal every morning, 1 cup of yogurt at lunch, and 1 cup of milk with her dinner. Does Janice need to include any more milk in her diet? Explain why or why not.

    _____

    _____

MAINTAINING SKILLS

Add or subtract.

1. $14.00
    − 8.75

2. $19.09
        6.78
    + 32.12

3. $24.09
    − 14.35

4. $44.45 + $4.45 = _____

Pacemaker ® Practical Mathematics for Consumers© Pearson Education, Inc. / Globe Fearon / Pearson Learning Group. All rights reserved.

11 **What Can I Do If I Do Not Eat Some Foods?**   **Exercise 59**

Lesson 11.2

Use the charts below to solve each problem. Show your work.

Amount of Protein a Person Needs Each Day			
Age in Years	Weight	Grams of Protein per Pound	Daily Protein Need in Grams
11–14	?	× 0.45	?
15–18	?	× 0.39	?
19+	?	× 0.36	?

Food	Amount of Protein
1 cinnamon bagel	8.72 grams
8 oz. skim milk yogurt	13.01 grams
1 cup orange juice	1.69 grams
1 cup kidney beans	13.44 grams

1. How much protein does a 16-year-old who weighs 125 pounds need each day?

2. Tess is 19 years old. She weighs 143 pounds. She consumed 14 grams of protein for breakfast and 25 grams of protein for lunch. How many more grams of protein must she consume to meet her daily need?

3. Fred is 13 years old. He weighs 105 pounds. He had a cinnamon bagel and 2 cups of orange juice for breakfast. He had an 8-ounce container of yogurt and a cup of kidney beans for lunch. How many grams of protein did he consume? How many more grams of protein must he consume to meet his daily need?

MAINTAINING SKILLS

Write each percent as a decimal.

1. 18% _____   2. 42% _____   3. 10.25% _____   4. 61% _____

Pacemaker ® Practical Mathematics for Consumers© Pearson Education, Inc. / Globe Fearon / Pearson Learning Group. All rights reserved.

Name _____   Date _____

Lesson 11.3

Use the charts below to solve each problem. Show your work.

Number of Calories in Food		
Food	**Serving Size**	**Calories**
Asparagus	1 cup	50
Butter	1 tbsp	102
Cauliflower	1 cup	25
Egg bagel	1 bagel	247
Hamburger	3 oz	230
Hamburger roll	1 roll	123

Number of Calories in Food		
Food	**Serving Size**	**Calories**
Mango	1 mango	135
Oatmeal cookie	1 cookie	65
Pork sausage	2 links	96
Potato pancake	1 pancake	207
Turkey	3 oz	132
Vanilla ice cream	$\frac{1}{2}$ cup	133

1. How many calories are in 1 cup of cauliflower?

2. How many calories are in 1 egg bagel with 2 tablespoons of butter?

3. How many calories are in 4 links of pork sausage?

4. How many more calories are in a 3-ounce hamburger than in a 3-ounce piece of turkey?

5. Kendall ate 3 ounces of turkey, 2 potato pancakes, 1 cup of asparagus, and 4 oatmeal cookies. How many calories did she consume?

6. Marla ate a half cup of vanilla ice cream for dessert. How many fewer calories would she have consumed if she had eaten an oatmeal cookie for dessert instead?

MAINTAINING SKILLS

Multiply.

1. $42 \times 12 =$ _____

2. $16 \times 4 =$ _____

3. $38 \times 7 =$ _____

4. $52 \times 21 =$ _____

Pacemaker ® Practical Mathematics for Consumers© Pearson Education, Inc. / Globe Fearon / Pearson Learning Group. All rights reserved.

11 **How Do You Burn Calories, and What Is Wrong With Fat, Salt, and Sugar?**   **Exercise 61**

Lessons 11.5 and 11.6

Use the chart below to solve Exercises 1–4.

Activity	Calories Burned per Hour
Washing dishes	137
Yoga	324

Activity	Calories Burned per Hour
Ice skating	372
Baseball	315

Find the calories you can burn with each activity.

	Activity	Total time doing the activity	Calories Burned
1.	Yoga	2 hours	
2.	Washing dishes	$\frac{1}{2}$ hour	
3.	Ice skating	$1\frac{1}{2}$ hours	
4.	Baseball	2 hours	

Solve. Show your work.

5. The average person should consume no more than 2,400 milligrams of sodium a day. Calvin ate 2 servings of chicken soup for lunch. Each serving contains 820 milligrams of sodium. How much sodium did he consume?

MAINTAINING SKILLS

Find the percent of each number.

1. 42% of $321 = _____

2. 2% of $45 = _____

3. 9.5% of $134 = _____

4. 22% of $179 = _____

Pacemaker ® Practical Mathematics for Consumers© Pearson Education, Inc. / Globe Fearon / Pearson Learning Group. All rights reserved.

12 ▸ What Do Food Labels Tell You?   Exercise 62

Lesson 12.1

Use the nutrition label on the right to answer each question.

Pete's Lentil Soup
Nutrition Facts
Serving Size 1 cup (241g)
Servings per container 2

Amount Per Serving	
Calories 140	Calories from fat 20
	% Daily Value*
Total Fat 2 g	3%
Saturated Fat 0 g	0%
Cholesterol 0 mg	0%
Sodium 750 mg	31%
Total Carbohydrate 22 g	7%
Dietary Fiber 7 g	28%
Sugars 2 g	
Protein 9 g	

Vitamin A 15%	Vitamin C 0%
Calcium 4%	Iron 20%

*Percent Daily Values (DV) are based on a 2,000 calorie diet.

1. How many servings are in a can of Pete's Lentil Soup?

2. What is the serving size of Pete's Lentil Soup?

3. How many calories are in one serving?

4. How many milligrams of salt are in one serving? (Hint: Sodium is salt.)

5. Is this soup a good source of vitamin C? Explain.

_____

_____

MAINTAINING SKILLS

Multiply or divide.

1. $\begin{array}{r} 321 \\ \times\, 0.28 \\ \hline \end{array}$

2. $\begin{array}{r} 36 \\ \times\, 0.04 \\ \hline \end{array}$

3. $1.2\overline{)420}$

4. $198 \times 0.61 = $ _____

Pacemaker ® Practical Mathematics for Consumers© Pearson Education, Inc. / Globe Fearon / Pearson Learning Group. All rights reserved.

Name _____ Date _____

Lesson 12.3

 Find which store offers the better buy.

Food	Gourmet Deli	Mike's Deli	Which Store Offers the Better Buy?
1. Grapes	$1.29 per pound	$3.00 for 3 pounds	
2. Ground beef	$4.25 for 4 pounds	$5.80 for 6 pounds	
3. Oatmeal cookies	$2.00 for 5 cookies	$0.50 for 1 cookie	
4. Cereal	$3.79 for 20 ounces	$1.99 for 10 ounces	

 Find which brand costs less per ounce.

Food	Nationally Advertised Brand	Store Brand	Which Brand Costs Less?
5. Sugar	$1.39 for 16 ounces	$0.89 for 14 ounces	
6. Grape juice	$2.99 for 48 ounces	$3.29 for 64 ounces	
7. Shampoo	$1.69 for 21 ounces	$1.99 for 24 ounces	

MAINTAINING SKILLS

Find the unit price. Round to the nearest cent.

1. $11.19 for 15 rolls of toilet paper

2. $3.29 for 24 ounces of shampoo

3. $2.49 for 45 tea bags

4. $0.99 for 15 pieces of gum

Pacemaker ® Practical Mathematics for Consumers© Pearson Education, Inc. / Globe Fearon / Pearson Learning Group. All rights reserved.

12 ▶ How Can Coupons Save You Money?   Exercise 64

Lessons 12.4 and 12.5

Solve Problems 1–3. Find each price when you use the coupon.

	Food	Regular Price	Value of Coupon	Price with Coupon
1.	Granola bars	$2.79	$0.65	
2.	Tomato sauce	$3.89	$0.40	
3.	Cake mix	$1.29	$0.30	

Solve each problem. Show your work. Use the coupon on the right for Problems 4 and 5.

4. Alisha buys 3 cans of Craig's Whole Tomatoes on 8/25/03. Could she use the coupon on the right? Explain.

Craig's Whole Tomatoes

Craig's WHOLE TOMATOES

SAVE **95¢**

When you buy two (2) 8-oz cans

1 coupon per customer   Offer expires 9/30/03

_____

_____

5. Alisha buys 3 cans of Craig's Whole Tomatoes. The price per can is $1.59. She uses the coupon. How much will she pay for 3 cans of tomatoes?

MAINTAINING SKILLS

Find the value of *x*.

1. $\dfrac{5}{15} = \dfrac{x}{30}$ 2. $\dfrac{x}{20} = \dfrac{4}{80}$ 3. $\dfrac{2}{x} = \dfrac{12}{36}$ 4. $\dfrac{5}{65} = \dfrac{15}{x}$

Pacemaker ® Practical Mathematics for Consumers© Pearson Education, Inc. / Globe Fearon / Pearson Learning Group. All rights reserved.

12 ▸ Are You a Wise Shopper?   Exercise 65

Lesson 12.6

**Read each statement. On the line, write *T* if the statement is true.
Write *F* if the statement is false.**

_____ **1.** You should find out what items are on sale before you make
your shopping list.

_____ **2.** You should buy processed snack foods.

_____ **3.** A calculator can help you when you shop.

Solve each problem. Show your work.

4. James is a cashier at the Gourmet Deli. He entered he wrong price on
his cash register. Instead of entering $3.70, he entered $7.30. How
much should James take off the bill to correct the mistake?

5. Andy is a cashier at Groceries & More. He entered the wrong price on
his cash register. Instead of entering $1.40, he entered $14.00. How
much should Andy take off the bill to correct the mistake?

MAINTAINING SKILLS
Circle the better buy.

1. 4 cans for $1.20   **2.** 18 ounces for $2.65

9 cans for $3.15   10 ounces for $1.80

3. 5 boxes for $5.50   **4.** 4 jars for $2.59

10 boxes for $11.00   12 jars for $6.57

Pacemaker ® Practical Mathematics for Consumers© Pearson Education, Inc. / Globe Fearon / Pearson Learning Group. All rights reserved.

13 ▶ How Do You Calculate Sales Tax on Items You Really Need?

Exercise 66

Lessons 13.1 and 13.2

Solve each problem. Show your work.

1. Mark gets a haircut every two weeks. He spends $15 and gives a $3 tip for each haircut. How much does he spend on haircuts in one year?

2. Luz spends about $150 a month on groceries. She realizes she spends about $25 a month on junk food. How much can she save a year if she stops buying junk food?

3. Dee bought three pairs of shoes. The shoes cost $97 altogether. Dee paid $104.76 including sales tax. How much did she pay in sales tax?

Find the sales tax for each item. Then find the total cost.

	Cost of Item	Sales Tax Rate	Amount of Sales Tax	Total Cost
4.	$64	8.25%		
5.	$120	6%		
6.	$78	5.5%		
7.	$15	7%		
8.	$39	5%		

MAINTAINING SKILLS

Write each decimal as a percent.

1. 0.175 _____
2. 0.21 _____
3. 0.535 _____
4. 0.012 _____

Pacemaker ® Practical Mathematics for Consumers© Pearson Education, Inc. / Globe Fearon / Pearson Learning Group. All rights reserved.

Name _____   Date _____

Lessons 13.3 and 13.4

Use the advertisement on the right for Exercises 1–3. Sales tax on all items is 6%. Round to the nearest cent if necessary.

1. Jack went shopping and bought 3 pairs of sweatpants and 4 T-shirts. How much did he spend? (Hint: Don't forget to add sales tax.)

STOREWIDE SALE

Woman's Bathing Suit	$28.99
Woman's Sweater	$29.99
Men's T-shirt	$9.99
Men's Sweatpants	$11.99
Men's Casual Pants	$19.99

2. Kevin has $100. He buys 4 pairs of casual pants. How much money does he have left? (Hint: Don't forget to add sales tax.)

3. Trina's favorite store is having a sale on sweaters: Buy one sweater at full price and get the second at half price. The retail price of the sweater is $29.99. If she buys 2 sweaters, how much will she pay? (Hint: Don't forget to add sales tax.)

Solve.

4. Kerri needs winter clothes. She went shopping and bought a sleeveless shirt and a bathing suit. Did she buy clothes that match her winter needs? Explain.

_____

_____

MAINTAINING SKILLS

Find the unit price. Round to the nearest cent if necessary.

1. $2.25 for 6 rolls of toilet paper

2. $8.26 for 3 pounds of chicken

3. $7.99 for 100 oz of liquid detergent

4. $1.59 for 2 pounds of bananas

Pacemaker ® Practical Mathematics for Consumers© Pearson Education, Inc. / Globe Fearon / Pearson Learning Group. All rights reserved.

13 ▷ What About Personal Care?   Exercise 68

Lesson 13.5

Solve each problem. Round to the nearest cent if necessary.
Show your work.

1. Diana bought 2 bottles of shampoo for $2.99 each, a bottle of conditioner for $2.79, and a tube of toothpaste for $2.59. Sales tax is 7.5%. How much did she pay for these items?

2. Dean bought a 3-pack of soap for $3.57, a new toothbrush for $1.49, dental floss for $0.99, and antiseptic ointment for $3.09. Sales tax is 6%. How much did he pay for these items?

3. Sandi has her hair colored at a beauty salon each month. She pays $48 plus a $10 tip. Sandi can buy hair dye for $11.99 and color her hair herself. If Sandi colors her own hair each month, how much will she save in one year?

4. Steve likes his dress shirts ironed. The laundry charges $1.50 to iron each shirt. Steve brings 18 shirts to the laundry each month. How much money will Steve save each month if he irons his own shirts?

MAINTAINING SKILLS

Compute.

1. $164
    × 12

2. 4)$172

3. $1,254
    + 123

4. $542
    − 96

5. $68 ÷ 2 = _____

6. $247.36 + $101.23 + $22.31 = _____

Pacemaker ® Practical Mathematics for Consumers© Pearson Education, Inc. / Globe Fearon / Pearson Learning Group. All rights reserved.

13 ▸ Is a Sale Item Always a Better Buy? Exercise 69

Lesson 13.6

Solve each problem. Show your work. Round to the nearest cent if necessary.

1. A package of 15 rolls of paper towels costs $10.99. How much do the paper towels cost per roll?

2. One pair of socks costs $3.99. The same socks are sold in a package of three pairs for $8.99. You were planning to buy three pairs of socks. How much do you save by buying the package?

3. A 4-pack of toothbrushes costs $9.99. The same toothbrush sells individually for $2.79. Which is the better buy?

4. You go out for pizza with two friends. You each plan to eat 2 slices. One slice costs $1.99. A small pizza, which has six slices, costs $9.99. How much will you and your friends save altogether by ordering the small pizza?

5. A 300-ounce bottle of liquid laundry detergent costs $18.99. A 200-ounce bottle of the same brand costs $15.99. Which is the better buy?

MAINTAINING SKILLS

Change each percent to a decimal.

1. 12% _____   2. 82% _____   3. 63% _____   4. 1.7% _____

Write each decimal as a percent.

5. 0.28 _____   6. 0.14 _____   7. 0.425 _____   8. 0.008 _____

Pacemaker ® Practical Mathematics for Consumers© Pearson Education, Inc. / Globe Fearon / Pearson Learning Group. All rights reserved.

Name _____ Date _____

Lesson 13.7

Use the advertisement below to solve each problem.
Show your work.

DVD Player

Originally $149.99, on sale for **$89.99***

plus 6% sales tax

*Sale price to the first 20 customers, this Sunday only.

1. Ari wants to buy a new DVD player. He sees the DVD player
   he wants advertised in an ad for Electronic City. It is on sale
   for $89.99. When Ari brings the DVD player to the cashier, the
   price is $149.99. Why doesn't Ari get the sale price? Explain.

   _____

   _____

2. Ari's friend saw the same advertisement for the DVD player.
   He got to the store on Sunday before it opened. Ari's friend
   was the first customer to buy the DVD player that day. How
   much did Ari's friend save?

3. How much is the sales tax on the sale price of the VCR? On
   the regular price?

MAINTAINING SKILLS

Compute. Round to the nearest cent.

1. $35.65 ÷ 5 = _____

2. 12)$143

3. $16.25 × 0.26 = _____

4. $1.25
   × 16

5. 16)$400.32

6. $455.30 ÷ 15 = _____

Pacemaker ® Practical Mathematics for Consumers© Pearson Education, Inc. / Globe Fearon / Pearson Learning Group. All rights reserved.

13 ▶ Can You Believe What You Read?   Exercise 71

Lesson 13.8

Solve each problem. Show your work. Round to the nearest cent if necessary.

1. Mary owns a nail salon. She buys nail polish for $1.25 a bottle. She marks up the price by 90%. How much does Mary charge per bottle of nail polish?

2. Ella buys a case of 36 bottles of juice for $21.60. She sells each bottle for $1.79. How much is the markup on each bottle of juice?

3. Patti makes beaded bracelets. She pays $0.75 for each piece of leather to string the beads. She pays $2 for the beads for each bracelet. Patti sells each bracelet for $10. How much is the markup on each bracelet?

4. Watson owns a clothing store. He buys T-shirts for $11 each. He marks up the price of each T-shirt by 50%. How much does he charge per T-shirt?

MAINTAINING SKILLS

Subtract.

| 1. | $57.25
−   7.37 | 2. | $19.00
− 17.21 | 3. | $57.36
−   5.21 | 4. | $5.51
− 3.33 |

Pacemaker ® Practical Mathematics for Consumers© Pearson Education, Inc. / Globe Fearon / Pearson Learning Group. All rights reserved.

Name _____   Date _____

Lesson 14.1

Use the Sale Calendar below to answer each question.

January	February	March	April	May	June
Home Goods Clothes Jewelry Shoes	Jewelry Coats Cosmetics	Clothes Shoes	Toys Clothes Shoes Coats Home Goods	Clothes Shoes Jewelry Cosmetics Home Goods	Clothes Shoes Home Goods
July	**August**	**September**	**October**	**November**	**December**
Home Goods	Clothes Swimsuits Shoes Home Goods	Clothes Shoes Coats Swimsuits	Cosmetics Home Goods	Toys Home Goods Jewelry Clothes Shoes	Cosmetics Home Goods Jewelry Clothes Shoes Toys

Sale Calendar

1. During which four months are cosmetics on sale?

   _____

2. Bernice decides in February that she needs some items for her new home. Which month is the earliest Bernice could buy her items on sale?

   _____

3. Jen buys 2 swimsuits on sale. The total cost of the swimsuits is $64.13. Jen gives the sales person four $20 bills. How much change will Jen receive?

MAINTAINING SKILLS

Subtract.

1. $124.25
    −   27.13

2. $26.25
    −   9.21

3. $167.89
    −   82.54

4. $53.24 − $17.25 = _____

Pacemaker ® Practical Mathematics for Consumers© Pearson Education, Inc. / Globe Fearon / Pearson Learning Group. All rights reserved.

Name _____   Date _____

14 ▸ How Do You Find the Sale Price?   Exercise 73

Lessons 14.2 and 14.3

Find each discount and each sale price. Write your answers
in the chart below.

	Retail Price	Percent of Discount	Amount of Discount	Sale Price
1.	$51	30%		
2.	$350	25%		
3.	$120	50%		
4.	$270	40%		
5.	$30	20%		

Solve each problem. Show your work.

6. Tony found a pair of boots at a factory outlet for 30% off the retail
   price of $89. How much is the discount?

7. Dorothy wants to buy a winter coat. The retail price of the coat is $159.
   The coal is on sale for 40% off. What is the sale price of the coat?

8. Fiona bought a new handbag for $16. The original retail price of the
   handbag was $32. What was the percent of discount on the handbag?

MAINTAINING SKILLS

Write each percent as a decimal.

1. 45% _____   2. 33% _____   3. 10% _____   4. 12% _____

5. 25% _____   6. 50% _____   7. 2% _____   8. 66% _____

Pacemaker ® Practical Mathematics for Consumers© Pearson Education, Inc. / Globe Fearon / Pearson Learning Group. All rights reserved.

14 ▶ How Do You Place a Catalog Order?   Exercise 74

Lesson 14.4

Solve each problem.

1. Find the total price of the order below. Fill in the price on the form.

Item Number	Catalog Page	Color	Item Size	Description	Quantity	Unit Price	Total Price of Items
2-2P	12	Red	L	Turtleneck	2	$11.99	

2. Omar wants to buy 4 pairs of blue pants in size medium. The retail price of the pants is $17.99 each. Fill in the order form below for Omar.

Item Number	Catalog Page	Color	Item Size	Description	Quantity	Unit Price	Total Price of Items
4-G	23						

3. Abby wants to buy 4 long-sleeve T-shirts from a catalog. The retail price is $12.99 for each shirt. The sale price is $9.99 each if you buy 3 or more shirts. What is the total price of the items?

    _____

4. Timmy wants to buy 8 pairs of socks from the catalog. The retail price is $3.99 each. The sale price is $1.99 each if you buy four or more pairs. How much will Timmy save altogether by buying the 8 pairs of socks?

    _____

MAINTAINING SKILLS

Find the percent of each number.

1. 13% of $231 _____
2. 29% of $690 _____
3. 40% of $96 _____

Pacemaker ® Practical Mathematics for Consumers© Pearson Education, Inc. / Globe Fearon / Pearson Learning Group. All rights reserved.

Pacemaker ® Practical Mathematics for Consumers© Pearson Education, Inc. / Globe Fearon / Pearson Learning Group. All rights reserved.

Name _____ Date _____

 14 **How Do You Find the Total Cost of Your Order?**

Lesson 14.5

Use the chart below to solve each problem.

Total Cost of Items	Shipping Cost
Up to $15.00	$3.95
$15.01 to $30.00	$7.95
$30.01 to $60.00	$11.95
Over $60.00	$16.95

1. Ali ordered a new jacket, hat, and gloves. The retail price is $40 for the jacket, $8.50 for the hat, and $7.50 for the gloves. How much is the shipping cost for Ali's order?

2. Bea ordered a blender and a tea kettle. The retail price of the blender is $32.99 and the tea kettle is $19.99. The sales tax is 7% on the items only. How much is the tax on Bea's order?

3. You place an order for 1 book and 2 CDs. The retail price is $13.75 for each CD and $8.75 for the book. The sales tax is 7% on the total cost with shipping. What is the total cost of your order including shipping and tax?

4. Randy orders a pair of sneakers, 3 T-shirts, and 2 pairs of shorts. The retail price of the sneakers is $29.99, the T-shirts are $7.00 each, and the shorts are $11.50 each. The sales tax is 8% on the total cost with shipping. What is the total cost of Randy's order, including shipping and tax?

MAINTAINING SKILLS

Solve each proportion.

1. $\dfrac{1}{5} = \dfrac{2}{x}$

2. $\dfrac{7}{x} = \dfrac{21}{36}$

3. $\dfrac{15}{3} = \dfrac{x}{6}$

4. $\dfrac{24}{36} = \dfrac{4}{x}$

Name _____ Date _____

 15 **What Kind of Transportation Will Save You Money?**

Lessons 15.1 and 15.2

Trina decided to buy a car. She wants to find the best buy possible. She created this chart using the prices from the car price guide.

Car	Invoice Price	MSRP
Car A	$9,025	$10,475
Car B	$10,150	$12,350
Car C	$11,100	$12,850
Car D	$13,450	$15,200

Use the chart above to solve each problem. Show your work.

1. What is the MSRP for Car B? _____

2. What is the difference between the invoice price and the MSRP for Car C?

3. Which car has the highest MSRP? The lowest? What is the difference between these two prices?

4. Trina finds a used car at a dealer for $6,100. The suggested retail price in the car price guide is $6,300. What is the difference between these two prices? Should Trina buy the car? Explain.

_____

_____

MAINTAINING SKILLS

Divide to find the percent. Round to the nearest whole percent.

1. $\frac{20}{80}$ _____

2. $\frac{15}{40}$ _____

3. $\frac{12}{27}$ _____

4. $\frac{5}{500}$ _____

5. $\frac{25}{75}$ _____

6. $\frac{16}{96}$ _____

Pacemaker ® Practical Mathematics for Consumers© Pearson Education, Inc. / Globe Fearon / Pearson Learning Group. All rights reserved.

15 ▶ What About Shopping for a Reliable Car?   Exercise 77

Lesson 15.3

The chart shows the retail prices for a sedan.

Retail Prices for a Sedan			
Car Dealer	Value Cars	Best Cars	Car World
Retail Price	$4,400	$5,230	$3,800

Use the chart above to solve each problem. Show your work.

1. Which dealer has the highest retail price? The lowest retail price?

2. How much more does the car cost at Best Cars than at Value Cars?

3. A car price guide lists $4,200 as the suggested retail price for the car. Which car dealer's price is lower than the suggested retail price from the car price guide? How much lower?

4. Value Cars offers an extended warranty for 1 year or until the car has been driven 60,000 miles, whichever comes first. When you buy the car, it already has been driven 46,341 miles. How many miles can you drive it in the next 12 months before the warranty expires?

MAINTAINING SKILLS

Multiply or divide.

1. $14.28
    ×   0.5

2. $7)\overline{\$357}$

3. $88.30 × 12 = _____

4. $66.12 ÷ 6 = _____

5. $6)\overline{733.80}$

6.   14.2
     × 7.5

Pacemaker ® Practical Mathematics for Consumers© Pearson Education, Inc. / Globe Fearon / Pearson Learning Group. All rights reserved.

15 ▶ How Do You Pay for a Car?   **Exercise 78**

Lesson 15.4

 Complete the chart below.

	Cost of Car	Percent of Down Payment	Amount of Down Payment	Amount of Loan
1.	$7,000	15%		
2.	$13,900	20%		
3.	$14,760	10%		
4.	$15,500	15%		
5.	$16,400	20%		

Solve each problem. Show your work.

6. Joy is buying a used car. She will make a 20% down payment. The price of the car is $4,800. How much will she put down? How much does Joy need to borrow to buy the car?

7. Gerry is buying a used car that costs $4,800. She trades in her old car for $1,500. She also makes a 10% down payment on the remaining price. How much will she need to borrow to buy the car?

8. Jarrell is buying a used car that costs $3,500. He makes a $2,000 down payment. What percent of the total cost is the down payment? Round to the nearest whole percent.

MAINTAINING SKILLS

Add or subtract.

1.	$50.02 + 8.41	**2.**	$61.09 − 52.13	**3.**	$14.45 + 12.32	**4.**	$79.57 − 16.22

Pacemaker ® Practical Mathematics for Consumers© Pearson Education, Inc. / Globe Fearon / Pearson Learning Group. All rights reserved.

Name _____ Date _____

Lesson 15.5

Billie Smith is buying a used car. Here is part of her contract.

BUYER: Billie Smith
            14 Transit Blvd, Freehold, NJ 07728
	SELLER: Car Town
	            11 Route 35, Eatontown, NJ 07724

NEW OR USED CAR: Used	MODEL YEAR: 1999
MAKE AND MODEL: 4-door sedan	VEHICLE IDENTIFICATION NUMBER:JH4DC46801X053484
ANNUAL PERCENTAGE RATE: 7%	NUMBER OF PAYMENTS: 36
PAYMENTS DUE MONTHLY STARTING: 3/01/03	AMOUNT OF PAYMENTS: $93.32

LATE PAYMENTS: A late charge of 10% of the payment is required if a payment is received 5 days after the due date.	
CASH PRICE OF CAR:	+ $4,600
AMOUNT OF SALES TAX (SALES TAX RATE = 7%):	+ $322
TOTAL OF OTHER CHARGES:	+ $100
AMOUNT OF DOWN PAYMENT:	− $2,000
UNPAID BALANCE: (AMOUNT OF LOAN):	= $3,022

Use Billie's contract above to answer each question.

1. How long is the term of Billie's auto loan in years? _____

2. How much did Billie give as the down payment? _____

3. What is the annual percentage rate on the loan? _____

4. What is the total purchase price of the car? (Hint: Add all
the costs listed on the contract above the down payment.)

MAINTAINING SKILLS

Find the percent of each number.

1. 9% of $80 _____   **2.** 3% of $129 _____

3. 65% of $589 _____   **4.** 12.5% of $800 _____

Pacemaker ® Practical Mathematics for Consumers© Pearson Education, Inc. / Globe Fearon / Pearson Learning Group. All rights reserved.

Name _____ Date _____

Lesson 15.6

Albert wants to get a new car. He compares the monthly payments for different interest rates.

Monthly Payments for a $1,000 Loan				
Interest Rate	12 Months	24 Months	36 Months	60 Months
7%	$86.53	$44.77	$30.88	$19.80
9%	$87.45	$45.68	$31.80	$20.76
10%	$87.92	$46.15	$32.27	$21.25
12%	$88.85	$47.08	$33.22	$22.24

Use the chart above to solve each problem. Show your work.

	Amount of Loan	Interest Rate	Term	Monthly Payment	Total Amount Paid
1.	$1,000	10%	2 years		
2.	$1,000	7%	1 year		
3.	$1,000	12%	5 years		
4.	$1,000	9%	3 years		

5. Albert has a $1,000 car loan. The loan has an interest rate of 12% and a term of 24 months. How much interest will Albert pay on the loan altogether?

MAINTAINING SKILLS

Compute.

1. $651.25
   + 37.42

2. $834.25
   − 26.57

3. $54
   × 18

4. $9\overline{)\$360}$

Pacemaker ® Practical Mathematics for Consumers© Pearson Education, Inc. / Globe Fearon / Pearson Learning Group. All rights reserved.

15 ▶ What About Leasing a Vehicle?   Exercise 81

Lesson 15.7

Complete the chart.

	Retail Price of Car	Percent of Depreciation	Amount of Depreciation	Residual Value of Car
1.	$9,900	35%		
2.	$10,800	40%		
3.	$11,500	45%		
4.	$12,500	40%		

Solve each problem. Show your work.

5. Marge's lease limits her mileage to 40,000 miles. When her lease ends, the car was driven 41,682 miles. The fee is $0.18 for each extra mile. How much does she owe for the extra miles?

6. Andy's lease limits his mileage to 30,000 miles. When his lease ends, the car was driven 33,821 miles. The fee is $0.14 for each extra mile. How much does he owe for the extra miles?

7. Dana leased a car for $229 a month for 5 years. How much will Dana pay each year for the lease? How much will she pay over 5 years?

MAINTAINING SKILLS

Find the percent of each number.

1. 38% of $333 _____   **2.** 56% of $100 _____

3. 14% of $70 _____   **4.** 40% of $120 _____

Pacemaker ® Practical Mathematics for Consumers© Pearson Education, Inc. / Globe Fearon / Pearson Learning Group. All rights reserved.

16 ▸ What About Car Insurance?   Exercise 82

Lessons 16.1 and 16.2

**Read each statement. If the statement is true, write *T* on the line.
If the statement is false, write *F* on the line. If the statement is false,
rewrite it so it is true.**

1. Liability insurance will cover your car in case of fire. _____

2. Collision insurance will cover the repair of your car _____
   if you are in an accident.

3. Medical coverage will pay your medical bills if you _____
   are in a car accident.

Use the chart to the right to solve Problems 4–6.

4. What is the difference in price between the
   highest liability rate and the lowest liability rate?

Liability Coverage 15/30/5	
Region	**Basic Annual Rate**
A	$470
B	$715
C	$300
D	$520

5. Which region has the highest rate?

6. Paul has 15/30/5 liability coverage on his car. What is the
   maximum amount the insurance company will pay for
   personal injuries if Paul is in a car accident?

MAINTAINING SKILLS

Add or subtract.

1.	$145.25	2.	$17.89	3.	$152.28	4.	$190.05
	101.54		4.20		− 16.02		− 29.30
	+ 571.01		+ 8.21				

5. $154.20 − $25.19 = _____

6. $219.02 + $16.28 = _____

Pacemaker ® Practical Mathematics for Consumers© Pearson Education, Inc. / Globe Fearon / Pearson Learning Group. All rights reserved.

Name _____ Date _____

Lessons 16.3 and 16.4

Solve each problem. Show your work.

1. Tyson has a collision deductible of $250. He was in a car accident and the repairs to his car will cost $488. How much will Tyson pay? How much will the insurance company pay?

2. Santo has a $150 comprehensive deductible. His car was damaged in a hurricane and it will cost $430 to fix the damage. How much will the insurance company pay?

3. The last time you changed your oil, the odometer read 14,389 miles. Now it reads 17,216 miles. How many miles have you driven since the last oil change?

4. When Omar checked his windshield washer fluid it was low. He went to an auto shop and bought a gallon of washer fluid for $1.25 and new windshield wipers for $13.49. There is 6% sales tax. How much did Omar spend including tax? Round to the nearest cent.

MAINTAINING SKILLS

Compute.

1. $12.37
   − 5.98

2. $16.54
   + 14.21

3. $389
   × 0.06

4. $13.25
   22.62
   + 8.25

5. $159 ÷ 4 = _____

6. $164 × 0.08 = _____

Pacemaker ® Practical Mathematics for Consumers© Pearson Education, Inc. / Globe Fearon / Pearson Learning Group. All rights reserved.

16 ▶ What About Car Repairs?

Exercise 84

Lesson 16.5

Use the car repair bill below to answer each question.

QTY.	PART	PRICE		DATE 3/12/04		ORDER NO.	WHEN PROMISED 3/13/04	PHONE 555-6767
1	Belt	41	27	YEAR & MAKE OF CAR—TYPE OR MODEL			ESTIMATE	SERIAL NO.
1	Gas filter	12	50	1999 Allison 220			$345	MOTOR NO.
1	Air filter	8	50	LICENSE NO.			MILEAGE	WRITTEN BY
				1VR-302			61,370	Pete
1	Brake shoe	60	50	DESCRIPTION OF WORK				AMOUNT
2	Brake drums	35	60	Change gas filter, air filter, & belts				80	00
				Change rear brakes				120	00

TOTAL PARTS ①		GAS, OIL & GREASE		CHECK BELOW		LABOR ONLY ②	
ESTIMATES ARE FOR LABOR ONLY, MATERIAL ADDITIONAL	LBS. GR.		LUBRICATE		PARTS	
	GALS. GAS		ENGINE OIL			
	QTS. OIL		TRANS.		GAS, OIL & GREASE	
I HEREBY AUTHORIZE THE ABOVE REPAIR WORK TO BE DONE ALONG WITH NECESSARY MATERIALS.	TOTAL GAS, OIL & GREASE		TOTAL SERVICE	TAX 6% ③	
	AUTHORIZED BY *Robert Young*			TOTAL ④	

1. What is the total cost of parts for Robert's car? Fill in the amount.

2. What is the total cost of the labor? Fill in the amount.

3. Tax is paid on parts. How much tax will Robert pay? Fill in the amount.

4. What is the total cost of the repair bill? Fill in the amount.

MAINTAINING SKILLS

Divide.

1. $4\overline{)\$360.28}$ 2. $5\overline{)\$130}$ 3. $11\overline{)\$231}$ 4. $8\overline{)\$64.16}$

Pacemaker ® Practical Mathematics for Consumers© Pearson Education, Inc. / Globe Fearon / Pearson Learning Group. All rights reserved.

17 ▶ How Much Does Recreation Cost?   Exercise 85

Lesson 17.1

A new ice-skating rink opened in Mason Village. The prices for Cool Skating are listed in chart.

Cool Skating
Prices are per person.

Skate Rental	$4.00
Lessons (per hour)	$25.00
OPEN SKATE:	
Adults	$7.50
Seniors (over 65)	$4.00
Students (18–23)	$6.50
Children (17 and under)	$5.50

Use the chart above to solve each problem. Show your work.

1. You went ice skating three times in January. You are an 18-year-old student. You rented skates each time you went. How much did you spend on ice skating in January?

2. Ada's mother takes Ada and four friends ice skating. Ada and her friends are all 10 years old. Ada and her mother have skates but the four friends need to rent skates. How much will Ada's mother spend on skating for the group?

3. Stan decides to take ice-skating lessons. How much will it cost to take a one-hour lesson once a week for a year?

MAINTAINING SKILLS

Find the percent of each number.

1. 60% of $120 _____   2. 1.5% of $30 _____   3. 18% of $439 _____

4. 30% of $19.90 _____   5. 20% of $210 _____   6. 2.5% of $92 _____

Pacemaker ® Practical Mathematics for Consumers© Pearson Education, Inc. / Globe Fearon / Pearson Learning Group. All rights reserved.

Name _____   Date _____

Lesson 17.2

Use the chart below to solve each problem.

Cool Skating Prices are per person.	Wednesday– Monday	Bargain Tuesdays
Skate Rental	$4.00	$2.50
OPEN SKATE:		
Adults	$7.50	$5.75
Seniors (over 65)	$4.00	$2.50
Students (18–23)	$6.50	$3.50
Children (17 and under)	$5.50	$2.75

1. Jackie is a 20-year-old student. She is planning to take her 8-year-old sister ice skating on Wednesday. They both need to rent skates. How much will Jackie save if they go on Tuesday instead of on Wednesday?

2. Mariela is planning to take her two children, ages 7 and 9, ice skating every Tuesday this month. Mariela has her own skates. The children need to rent skates. How much will Mariela spend for four weeks of ice skating this month?

3. Boris is a 20-year-old student. He took his father ice skating Friday night. They both rented skates. How much would Boris have saved if they went ice skating on a Tuesday instead of on a Friday?

MAINTAINING SKILLS

Estimate each sum or product. Round to the nearest ten.
Then add or multiply.

1. $41 + 17	2. $16 + 7	3. $11.17 × 9.63	4. $18.74 × 9.13

Pacemaker ® Practical Mathematics for Consumers© Pearson Education, Inc. / Globe Fearon / Pearson Learning Group. All rights reserved.

Name _____ Date _____

17 ▸ How Can Comparing Prices Save You Money?

Exercise 87

Lesson 17.3

Supreme Driving Range offers three different-size baskets of balls for golfers to use on the driving range. Once a golfer uses all the balls in a basket, he or she pays for a new basket of golf balls.

Supreme Driving Range	
Small bucket of golf balls	$7
Medium bucket of golf balls	$10
Large bucket of golf balls	$13

Use the advertisement above to solve each problem.

1. Last week you went to the driving range three times. You bought a medium bucket of golf balls each visit. How much did you spend?

2. Suzie goes to the driving range four times a month. She gets a large bucket of golf balls each time. How much will Suzie spend on golf balls in one year?

3. Mitch saved $75 to buy a new golf club. He bought a club for $65. Then he went to the driving range. Mitch bought two large buckets of golf balls. Does he have enough money left over after buying the club to pay for the golf balls? If not, how much more money does he need?

MAINTAINING SKILLS

Compute.

1. $59.20
    + 1.58

2. $35.00
    − 21.75

3. $59 ÷ 4 = _____

4. $18.61
    ×   12

5. 17)$3,400

6. $29.00 + $16.50 + $18.00 = _____

Pacemaker ® Practical Mathematics for Consumers© Pearson Education, Inc. / Globe Fearon / Pearson Learning Group. All rights reserved.

Name _____ Date _____

 17 ► **How Can You Budget for Recreation Costs?**

Exercise 88

Lesson 17.4

Joan wants to buy her own snorkeling equipment. She made a list of the items she needs and the price of each item.

Snorkeling Equipment	
Flippers	$49.50
Snorkel	$22.90
Mask	$27.60
Vest	$38.00

Use the chart above to solve each problem. Show your work.

1. Joan wants to buy all the items on her list. There is 8% sales tax on these items. How much will she spend on snorkeling equipment?

2. If Joan saves $15 a week, how long will it take her to save enough money to buy all the equipment? (Hint: Round up to the next whole week.)

3. Joan goes snorkeling four times during her vacation. She pays $18 each time. How much does Joan spend on snorkeling that week?

4. Joan finds a place where she can go snorkeling once a month. It costs $15 per snorkeling trip. How much will she spend on snorkeling trips in one year?

MAINTAINING SKILLS

Find the percent of each number. Round to the nearest whole percent.

1. $12 out of $96 _____

2. $38 out of $250 _____

3. $758 out of $2,642 _____

4. $0.10 out of $1,000 _____

Pacemaker ® Practical Mathematics for Consumers© Pearson Education, Inc. / Globe Fearon / Pearson Learning Group. All rights reserved.

Name _____ Date _____

 How Do You Use a Road Map? **Exercise 89**

Lesson 18.1

Use the map below to find each distance.

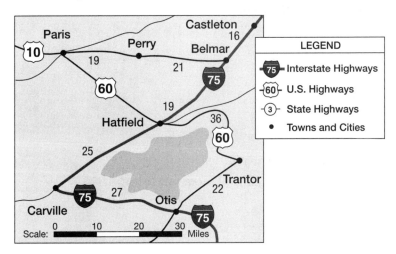

1. How many miles is it from Castleton to Hatfield on Interstate Highway 75?

2. Which road would you take to get from Carville to Belmar?

3. Melissa is driving from Carville to Otis to pick up a friend. They will then go to Trantor for the day. What roads will Melissa take? How many miles will she drive from Carville to Trantor?

4. Jason is traveling from Otis to Belmar. Which route is the shortest route? How many miles is this route? (Hint: There are two possible ways to go.)

MAINTAINING SKILLS

Change each decimal to a percent.

1. 0.25 _____ 2. 0.013 _____ 3. 0.30 _____ 4. 0.05 _____

Pacemaker ® Practical Mathematics for Consumers© Pearson Education, Inc. / Globe Fearon / Pearson Learning Group. All rights reserved.

18 ▸ How Long Will the Trip Take?   **Exercise 90**

Lesson 18.2

Use the chart below to solve each problem. Show your work.
Round up to the next whole hour if you need to.

Road	Speed Limit
Interstate highway	65 mph
County road	45 mph
Local road	25 mph

1. Carson drives 230 miles on interstate highways, 75 miles on county roads, and 27 miles on local roads. About how many hours is Carson driving?

2. Donna drives 120 miles on interstate highways, 30 miles on county roads, and 10 miles on local roads. About how many hours is Donna driving?

3. Dan is a truck driver. He drives about 500 miles a day on interstate highways. About how many hours does Dan drive each day?

4. Max is planning a trip. He will drive 1,200 miles on interstate highways. He wants to drive only 7 hours a day. About how many days will Max's trip take?

MAINTAINING SKILLS

Divide.

1. $4\overline{)\$168}$ 2. $16\overline{)\$6,432}$ 3. $5\overline{)\$350.05}$ 4. $3\overline{)\$57}$

5. $\$819 \div 9 =$ _____   6. $\$1,625 \div 10 =$ _____

Pacemaker ® Practical Mathematics for Consumers© Pearson Education, Inc. / Globe Fearon / Pearson Learning Group. All rights reserved.

18 ▶ How Much Will Gasoline Cost?   Exercise 91

Lesson 18.3

Find each gas mileage. Round to the nearest mile per gallon.

	Number of Miles Traveled	Number of Gallons of Gas	Gas Mileage
1.	337 miles	13 gallons	
2.	302.6 miles	16 gallons	
3.	427 miles	12 gallons	

Find the cost of gas for each trip.

	Total Miles	Gas Mileage	Price of Gas per Gallon	Cost of Gas for Trip
4.	756 miles	28 miles per gallon	$1.40	
5.	300 miles	20 miles per gallon	$1.69	
6.	224 miles	32 miles per gallon	$1.27	

Solve. Show your work.

7. Tamara and 2 friends will drive 1,500 miles on their summer vacation. The car they are driving gets about 25 miles per gallon. Gas costs $1.32 a gallon. About how much will gasoline cost for the trip? The friends split the cost of gasoline equally. About how much does each friend pay for gasoline?

MAINTAINING SKILLS

Find the percent of each number.

1. 9% of $45 _____

2. 20% of $68 _____

3. 6% of $987 _____

4. 40% of $434.65 _____

Pacemaker ® Practical Mathematics for Consumers© Pearson Education, Inc. / Globe Fearon / Pearson Learning Group. All rights reserved.

Name _____ Date _____

Lesson 18.4

Solve each problem. Show your work. Round to the nearest cent.

1. Paul is going away for four nights. He finds a four-star hotel for $70 a night, not including tax. The tax rate is 5%. How much will Paul spend for the hotel, including tax?

2. Corinna has a coupon for $8 off any dinner that is $21.95 or more. The sales tax is 8%. If Corinna chooses a dinner for $23.50 how much will she pay, including tax? How much is a 20% tip on the cost of the meal, not including tax?

3. Maureen is going to visit her family for one week. The bus takes 14 hours. It costs $77.60. A plane ticket costs $179. It will take only 2 hours. How much more would it cost to fly? How much shorter is the flight than the bus ride?

MAINTAINING SKILLS

Add or subtract.

1. $352.14
  − 32.18

2. $11.25
 21.44
 + 9.21

3. $124.54
 − 18.31

4. $10.00
 + 5.15

5. $186.24 − $93.02 = _____

6. $29.08 + $16.32 = _____

Pacemaker ® Practical Mathematics for Consumers© Pearson Education, Inc. / Globe Fearon / Pearson Learning Group. All rights reserved.